Southern Messenger Poets

Dave Smith, Editor

OTHER WORKS BY REGINALD GIBBONS

Poetry

Roofs Voices Roads

The Ruined Motel

Saints

Maybe It Was So

Fiction

Five Pears or Peaches

Sweetbitter

Translation

Selected Poems of Luis Cernuda

Guillén on Guillén: The Poetry and the Poet
(edited and translated with Anthony L. Geist)

Criticism

William Goyen: A Study of the Short Fiction

Sparrow

Sparrow

new and selected poems

*for Charles, with
every good hope*

REGINALD GIBBONS

Reg

2002

LOUISIANA STATE UNIVERSITY PRESS   *Baton Rouge and London*   1997

Copyright © 1969, 1973, 1974, 1976, 1978, 1979, 1980, 1981, 1983, 1985, 1986, 1989, 1990, 1991, 1993, 1994, 1995, 1996, 1997 by Reginald Gibbons
All rights reserved
Manufactured in the United States of America
First printing
06 05 04 03 02 01 00 99 98 97   5 4 3 2 1

Designer: Michele Myatt Quinn
Typeface: Bembo
Typesetter: Impressions Book and Journal Services
Printer and binder: Thomson-Shore, Inc.

Library of Congress Cataloging-in-Publication Data

Gibbons, Reginald.
    Sparrow : new and selected poems / Reginald Gibbons.
        p.   cm.—(Southern messenger poets)
    ISBN 0-8071-2232-7 (alk. paper).—ISBN 0-8071-2233-5 (pbk. :
alk. paper)
        I. Title.   II. Series.
PS3557.I1392S67   1997
811'.54—DC21   97-23555
                                                                   CIP

Poems herein have been selected from *Maybe It Was So* (University of Chicago Press, 1991); *Saints* (Persea Books, 1986); *The Ruined Motel* (Houghton Mifflin, 1981); *Roofs Voices Roads* (Quarterly Review of Literature, 1979). The author wishes to thank the editors of the following publications, in which some of the new poems, or versions of them, first appeared: *Alaska Quarterly Review, American Poetry Review, Atlantic Monthly, Many Mountains Moving, Notre Dame Review, Ontario Review, Poetry East, Quarterly Review of Literature, Southern Review, Switched-On Gutenberg.*
    "White Beach" was reprinted in *Best American Poetry 1996.*
    "Desterrado" was commissioned by Princeton University for Charter Day, October 15, 1996, and originally bore the epigraph "Firestone Library, Princeton University."
    "Sparrow" was reprinted in *Pushcart Prize XXII: Best of the Small Presses.*

Again for C.

This charm is green in the red world.
Low leaf that opens anyway
among dry shells, by a hard road.
In the chained world, this charm is free.

A private charm against good-byes
when you and I release each other—
the kiss we give, these orphan cries
we swallow, this turning to a feather.

I kiss your mouth, you kiss me back:
this charm's a statement and reply—
and a seed, a wedge, a way to take
some change into our work today.

The kiss is hidden in the border of the night.
Leaf that is ours, love that is green,
give all of us more life, more bright
hours and days together again.

And for K. and S., who best changed my world
And remembering
    W. G.
    T. D. P.
    T. McG.
    D. D.

CONTENTS

New Poems

Desterrado, late 1960s   3

White Beach   5

Sparrow   9

Folk Saying   11

City   12

View from a Western Hilltop   16

Fervors   17

   Hope

   Worship

   Fear

   Adventure

   Rage

   Love

   Admiration

   Quiet

Image of a Young Man, c. 1994   25

With Wings / *Con alas*   27

St. Valentine's Eve   30

From *Maybe It Was So* (1991)

The Affect of Elms   39

A Rememberer   40

Long-Ago Yaupon   41

Stars   42

Lovers   43

Hark   44

Poem   45

From a Paper Boat   46

An Explosion   57

Madrid   59

Hide from Time   60

Teacher   62

From *Saints* (1986)

Eating   65

Elsewhere Children   67

Make Me Hear You   70

Two Kinds of Singing   72

Her Love   74

That Phone Call   75

April to May   77

Away from You   79

Saints   80

    1 The Blue Dress

    2 A Personal Need

    3 Where the Green Gulf

    4 Just Crazy Thinking

    5 Read This

    6 Sermon of the New Preacher

    7 Witness

    8 The Snarling Dog

    9 Cash or Turtle or Heaven

    10 In the Violent Ward

From *The Ruined Motel* (1981)

In the Kingdom   113

The Voice of Someone Else   116

Breath   117

The Days   118

"Luckies"   119
Lentils   120
The Letter   122
Small Elegy   124
At Noon   125
Hoppy   126
The Ruined Motel   127
Prayer Before Bathing   130
Those Who Are Gone   131

From *Roofs Voices Roads* (1979)

Two Promises   135
Betrayal   136
Dusk   138
In a Study over a Stage   140
Pine Island   141
Buddy   142
Behind the Mountain   144
In Memoriam Ezra Loomis Pound   145
An Archaeology of the Future   146

New Poems

DESTERRADO, LATE 1960s

From the mouth of the aging professor, spoken in his exiled Castilian,
histories, episodes and anecdotes of his native country,
sunny clarities of phrase to describe dank imprisoning shadows,
to describe a few rationalists and educators, long ago already,
unbuilding stone by stone
long-established walls and windowless superstitions
and building new practice,
to describe a few philosophers and poets who tried
to break open the sealed certainties
of bulls and confession and whorehouses and child-beating;
his dark eyes looking at the past, not at us;
and the language-shaped curve of his face,
of his mouth that calmly explained to us—
mouth that had denounced the fascist uprising and praised the Spanish
    Republic;
mouth that remembered the victims;
mouth, I imagined, that had lied to border guards somewhere, once upon a
    time;
mouth that had pressed against the mouth of his young wife
perhaps only the night before the seminar, perhaps only that very morning;
mouth that gave up his burning cigarette to his small émigré hand;
hand, languorous or weary, that returned, holding the cigarette,
to rest on the table as his words glittered in the close air;
hand that when even smaller had been led under nineteenth-century trees
and around very old stone corners and down narrow streets
the sun could not attain and across broad avenues
in stark dusty summer or in rain-wet wine-scented winter,
in days of mule carts and horse carriages before the assaults and attacks of
    velocity,
all of that in a changed realm he had not seen for thirty years;
hand that had offered, I imagined, a dubious passport to border guards
    somewhere;
hand, I imagined, that had never struck his own child;
hand that wrote an antiquated cursive script and sometimes corrected proofs;
hand that had pressed against the uncovered egalitarian breast of his young
    wife

perhaps only the night before the seminar, perhaps only that very morning
when she had brought him his memorious black coffee;
hand like my own hand writing quickly what I could not entirely grasp,
like my younger brother's hand, which had struck at me with futile blows of
    self-defense,
like my mother's hand, writing as big a small check as she could,
like my father's hand,
which had come from some remote labor to clasp my hand as I had said
    good-bye.

White Beach

for D. Y.

Once in a while in the sounds of wind and voices
there is some story of us, and the sound of making love

when both persons are inside it. I didn't know that, then,
when we all were too young to know because even if

we had done it we had never yet been inside it.
At the Freeport beach each of us was his body, or hers;

it was as though, forced or willing, we were put on display to each other
by our species, which was sorting us for reproduction.

Sunburned and tired, we were on our way home
in the dark after my friend's front teeth were gone,

lost for all time in the Gulf when his surfboard
jumped away from him and then right away found him again

as he was flailing under that last wave in the summer-late dusk,
wave he shouldn't have ridden anyway. Even so,

he was driving his own car because no one else
was allowed to, but his bleeding had stopped

and the rest of us were already forgetting
that his whole head was throbbing,

we were thinking about each other's bodies,
things we wanted to see in each other.

We were on the unavoidable straight road
through a shantytown where drivers coming back to the city

want to speed up but have to slow down this night
because of the confusion, because drunk on beer and heartache

some young black men are throwing or threatening to throw
bottles, stones, bricks at us, at every car that passes.

Shouts and taunts. We get through that,
it quiets us, but in other cars some of the other white boys

have had enough beer to want to stop and fight
and their girlfriends hang onto them pleading no and love.

And some of the black boys are held back too
by young women with inescapable thoughts of aftermath.

Hurt, harm, what might, what certainly would, be lost
when our kind convulsed against each other.

(And those who were hurt were often
heroes for it, loved more than others.)

Mile by mile, much too fast, now, we return
to late-night avenues and three-high overpasses.

Hot and dank and subtropical, our half-raised city
is all pretense at reality, the buildings stand

beside the freeways as if they really are solid,
we speed through the late emptiness

of the summer night concocting our alibis
and explanations, in case. We think

about it again and again—we held our breath,
we were taut with fright when we realized what

was happening and cars ahead of us began to stop
and we had to stop and we didn't know that someone

might not run right up to us and heave a brick in or worse;
and one of us already was hurt (and loved for it).

Didn't we know it wasn't at all the same as the other way around—
when white boys like us went out at night to drive

through city wards and outlying shantytowns,
brandishing baseball bats from the open windows

of their cars, front and back, their hands
in a furious grip, their mouths taunting. . . .

Coolly he swerved to follow the off-ramp, drifting wide
just the right amount, then he cut the turn at the light hard,

the girl he thought he was going to marry
thrown close against him, holding onto him

as he raced his own pain down the last streets of dark houses
for the first drop-off, who was kissing someone

in the back seat, pressing one hand against a thigh,
the other inside it. And in the sound of the night air

blowing into the car and in the injured scents
of green and pink, of fishwater and beer

and mown weeds and waxleaf ligustrum and sweat
and suntan lotion and lipstick and skin

and damp clothes and sea salt and hot paving tar
there was something like the smell of human love and hate

when people are really inside them.
This much I think we all of us did know.

SPARROW

In the town streets
pieces of the perishing world
Pieces of the world coming into being

The peculiar angle at which a failing gutter descends
from a house-eave; a squirrel's surviving tattered nest of leaves
woven into a high bare crook of an elm tree
    (the last one alive on this street);

the small bright green leafing out of that elm;
a man shaking coins in a dry Coke-cup and saying
Small change, brother? Small change?;
                    a woman
in scuffed white running shoes and a fine suit hurrying
down the street with a baggy briefcase that must have
papers and her purse and her good shoes inside it
Perhaps a small pistol

Gusts rattle the half-closed upstairs window
    in the old office building that's going to be torn down

Skittering across the sidewalk, a scrap of paper
    with someone's handwriting on it, in pencil
A message that will arrive

Things in themselves

A few minutes of seeing
An exalting

Or a few minutes of complete shelter
A protectedness, a brief rest from the changes

Sparrow moments

       ~

But this emblem I take from the world—
able, fussing, competing
at the feeder, waiting on a branch,
sudden in flight, looping and rushing, to another branch,
quick to fight over mating and quick at mating,
surviving winter on dry dead seed-heads of weeds
and around stables and garbage and park benches,
near farms and in deep woods,
brooding in summer-hidden nests—house sparrow,

song sparrow, fox sparrow, swamp sparrow,
field sparrow, lark sparrow, tree sparrow, sage sparrow,
white-throated sparrow of the falling whistled song
that I hear as a small reassurance—

Would my happiness be that the sparrow not be emblem—
that it be in my mind only as it is outside of my mind, itself,
that my mind not remove it from itself
into realms of forms and symbolic thinking?

My happiness, that is, my best being

Words like branches and leaves,
or words like the birds among
the branches and leaves?

They take wing all at once
The way they flee makes flight look like exuberance not fear
They veer away around a house-corner

FOLK SAYING

Because, having cooked food over a fire,
   when we eat outside among trees
   eating together can seem again a ceasing
   of fear and anger, and therefore of war;
because to do this even in our day
   is therefore to make of eating a ceremony
   that leads us to be more civil to one another
   and to think of those at the mercy of hatred;
because at such a ceremony it is well
   to invite one's enemy—that is,
   whoever is not oneself, and even oneself—
   to approach without fear or anger,
and it is good to offer, instead of enmity,
   all hospitable care
   for the sake of peace, not advantage,
but also out of pity for us all
   in our weak fearfulness and anger,
   our fragility (we almost collapse
   at the crackle of a fire,
and even a hand can make blood
   run out of us);
because it is an honor and an occasion
   when what is in us can be loved;
   and you are lovely;
because of all these thoughts,
   and unwitting inheritances of custom,
   and the pleasure sometimes of old set ways
   of saying things,
when we two stand at the dwindling fire after eating,
and the deepening night is the shadow
of ancient horses and the fire
breathes up a gray acrid banner
that reaches this way and that till it finds you
and includes you and you half shut your eyes
and half turn away, I say to you:
Smoke follows the fair.

CITY

Again in this early spring
the scents of wet earth and
new green arrive
like hesitant recruits in the old
neighborhoods. The handsome
and ugly brick buildings
whisper their forgotten war
stories to the acidic city
air night and day,
in snow and sun, presiding
over streets named for
forgotten local Shermans
and Grants who used to gather
with their admirers in the old
forerunners of these present-
day eateries and bars—
the insider reticence, the cool
iced tea and beer in summer,
shots and hot coffee
in winter, among the ex-
officers and enlisted men,
soldiers and sailors who did
something for the Union. . . .

Then came the Great Fire,
then the double-zero year,
then another war, electricity—
safer than gas—and automobiles
got heavier and faster,
the horses gone, the veterans
of the Great War came home

looking for work, worked,
some of them kept tiny

gardens on their back landings
and in window boxes. . . .

Clean-shaven, short-
haired young men
in jackets and ties who had
graduated or not from
the old high school
made lives or lost them
on the job or in the big
next war, the next
and the next. Finally the settlement
house that had seen off
a whole long-ago regiment
closed, the Wobblies' hall
became a rock club,
the grocery store small offices,
the theater a maze of video
rentals, comics, pillows,
candy and jeans and shoes,
the church is vacant, someone
removed the small memorial
tablet that remembered eighty
or one hundred bronze
names from this unpolished parish.

On a Saturday morning in
the old hardware store
with scuffed wooden floors,
an old man helps me—
so present to me that he
fully commits me
to his cause, which is only
that he knows of or will
discover everything that might
be asked for in such

a store: a man's kind
knowledge. He finds
exactly the few oddments
I am seeking and then
with a miniature key in his hand
he goes to a glass cabinet,
he unlocks it and reaches in
to get for me the small
knife I want to buy.

My little daughter was with me
that day, he smiled at her
and asked her where she
was going to school and when
she told him he said
that was where he'd gone,
too, when he was a boy.
"That one, and then the middle
school, *and* the high school, too.
But I wasn't smart—I left
the high school before
I graduated," he was saying.
"Went into the army.
Funny thing is,
my son did exactly the same
in World War II."
He handed me the knife.
"I had three sons
in World War II."
He returned the key to his pocket.
"Two of them didn't come back."
Without making any
sound he started to cry
and turned half away
to half touch at his eyes
with his thick fingertips. "It killed
my wife. Took nine years

to do it, but it killed her."
He looked at us again.
Recovering.

       Shying. "Anything
else you need?" He touched
my child's hair for an instant.
"I grow tulips. Have
a thousand of them now.
My whole back yard's
tulips, the front yard, too.
The best ones are from
Holland, you know."
              How
often does the defining
pain still come
through him?
       He bent down
toward the small girl,
my child, and said to her,
"You'd like seeing them. They're
pretty little fellows."

VIEW FROM A WESTERN HILLTOP

after Chang K'o-Chiu

The wind saws itself against the dull blades of red granite ridges
Over the jagged humps and tumbled crags of the low peaks it scrapes itself
It riffles the rainwater pools in stone hollows

The rock-perches are splashed white with hawk-scat
and with a quartz-cracking lichen, yellow-orange as a flame

Below, a harrier glides up the dry lake bed over
dead shells, savage little burrs, a delicate sharp-toothed skull

The wind tears downward at itself and rushes into voice through
the spikey scrub-oak leaves

The rattlesnake is wild
The spider is wild
The lion is wild

What makes such wildness tame
is memories of what men have done

FERVORS

1 Hope

Cold wind in northern April,
nothing green yet

An orphaned world

A deep repeated note, which
if I could only hear it
would sound I am sure like
it was struck on a harp

When I was walking
I happened to look up into the bare trees

Only from where I was, just then,
could I have seen the high
more-white-than-white snow
in a shallow raw trough of pale wood
where a big limb had been
broken off by the weight of ice
during the winter we had almost left behind

A little pillow
of snow when the late snow
everywhere else had melted

A cold purity

And inquiring from a buffeted higher branch
pitching in the wet spring wind, a crow

2 Worship

I saw him walk down to the pew
where she was sitting at the aisle

I saw him touch her shoulder
carefully, as if it had thorns

I saw her turn her surprised face up to him

I saw him lean down toward her
and in front of everyone
just as the service was about to begin
and the organist was finishing the introit
I saw him kiss her on the mouth

Then he turned and walked back
up the aisle and out of the sanctuary

He wasn't one to come to services very often

She sang the first hymn so loud

My God, her lips

3 Fear

My father's dead, my head hurts.
Is it heed that hurts?

I've had nightmares in this head all day long.
I wouldn't want you to say them. Or sing anything.

To drink of running water seems too much a miracle.
To sit down now to a meal seems too unreal.

Families broken at the heart of hell; camps; famine;
and hell at the heart of the family:

the pictures in my head won't go away, won't disappear,
but I feel that if I say exactly what I see, they'll suffer even more.

On rampage, predatory men; on rampage, both remembered and forgotten
    gods.
Shiva and Mars; ogresses and demons; murderous demagogues.

Shatterings; laughter behind the trigger; rulers over the ruled.
And for entertainment, guns and seductions all day, all night, all world.

At home, my head hurts—my father's deed, my mother's failed word.
She tried! He said he was not too ill to be loved; and he died.

Our hands have been let go. Our daily dread.
You are all waiting, but I can hardly cut this bread.

4 Adventure

Fucking a middleweight boxer, lying under
his body as hard as wood
till it's softened, lying on you,
your thrill the wonder of his being
gentle, careful, tender with you when
he could be a little harder,
that would be OK, he could push
you a little farther, but nothing
like hit you, no way, he could have hit you,
I'm sorry, already and hurt you badly but
that's not him at all, he's completely
the opposite—yes, quick and determined and even
after being hit in the face still smart in the ring
but in bed quiet, slow, needing encouragement
and yet you know there's always that chance
that that's the real him, that other one whom
you do adore, you see the look in the eyes
of the men and women watching him fight,
they love him or don't care about him or hate him
but they look, they watch, he has
the courage to get up in there and try to hurt
without being too hurt, with his own and only body
and no weapons, no place to hide, just
his gloved hands, these hands that grasp
your shoulder, palm your breast, move
over you and into you, you pull him down
onto you, you pull him to you with every
bit of your strength that's small compared to his
but enough to make him gasp and give up,
he won't win this one, if it's a contest
and maybe it is, you will, and he could
have hurt you any time, any time, but he didn't.

5 Rage

after Carlos Drummond de Andrade

You war against the depraved world.
You have heard the call, from the center of what is true, to act.
You believe, you have faith, that what is human
and divine has been disposed for you and your people.

In this city that you enter, other peoples' heroes crowd the parks,
extolling the wrong virtues and visions that are false.
On horseback one points toward the museum of art.
The libraries echo with ungodly mockery and scorn.

You love the explosive streets—anything is possible.
And when you sleep, you dream of putting on layer after layer after layer of
    clothing.
Waking returns you to the task of destroying those whom you hate.
Among their indecipherable entertainments, their unavailing claims, they sell
    to you the tools of their own destruction.

They are already dead. They will never understand the truth
that you live. Even some of them know
their measures are feeble, their benedictions are lies.
They conceal, they pretend, they defile, they lapse.

You are humble, you submit to your God and your cause.
You will not allow the years to pass without some righteous blow.
You will not accept that nothing can be done you can
bring down their city you can raise your tower of triumphant smoke.

6 *Love*

Sometimes bitter, because insufficient to fulfill
all the hopes it raises, this
pairing off. But sweet, given—
by whom or what?—our mutual acknowledgments
and permissions. We make a story
for ourselves: after our exile
from each other, after our refuge
in each other, after the intensities and altitudes
of the disclosing moments:

when we stood beside a tangerine tree on an early day
that lit us with light reflected off the ocean far from
some home we hadn't yet found, for instance,

and when you put three coins in my hand then
I reached to place them in the sacred palm of another man
waiting for us to pay for our passage through a gate,

and when we sat together at the open window
of a secret cabin overlooking water—
                                        was that
yesterday or will it be tomorrow, all

our episodes in this history that's just ours?

7 Admiration

The autumn day dark early

Windy rain approaching from the prairie

like a stranger from the prairie

And down between great buildings on the shadowed city street someone
sheltered in the cold chapel of an unused doorway
with another blind paper cup at his feet
was playing on a saxophone
he had brought with him in a shopping bag
the classics of improvisation

                          the great tunes
the riffs of his tradition
                the changes

handed down again just now by him

And in the pushing wind, the certainty of rain, soon—
who stopped for a moment to listen and pitched
his own voice to the blue note
and a few coins into the cup?

8 Quiet

I was not disciplined enough
to rise at dawn, but when
I rose I left behind
rooms of furious thinking
so that I could watch,
atop this former mountain,
now a tumbled-down
small hill, the sun
reach into the lowest
least bush: it was
a last path that I climbed
to get to this ancient summit
hidden out in the grass-and-granite
open from the closed
customary places of thought.

So:
Wind pushing the grass
in flowing waves. Slow
brown wingbeats of a hawk.
And the lake below empties
itself of darkness like a mind
quieting.
   There is no sound
of sound.
   Only an echo
of what was not heard,
echo of that which
bells or chimes were long ago
invented to imitate.

Image of a Young Man, c. 1994

> The belly of the weapon is full of all that it has eaten.
> —Mazisi Kunene

In the television tidings of today
his brief staring at a camera becomes
a staring at us, without his knowing
who or where we will be
Then comes another image, unrelated. . . .

The dirt in your hand was your country

Can you believe now that with your body-builder friends
you used to play speed chess between outdoor sets of heavy lifting
and you used to wear American jeans and say *California*
and sometimes you used to go with Lidija to Suleyman's quiet house,
she was so beautiful in the afternoon,
and make love in his bedroom and sleep a little while
and you thought your world was waiting for you?

Your hands are as light as dead birds
and are still too heavy for you to lift
Your skin is tight over all your countable bones
At the bottom of you lie exploded bedrooms,
wrecked bodies, burnt expectations, imaginary indictments. . . .
The cold well water is poisoned
The orchards machine-gunned

In front of all of you starved for your own lives
a guard walks by outside the fence: immense, robust, filled
with the unassailable surplus of his life;
free, unpenalized, immune. . . .
He went with a group of other guards
to Lidija
He went to her with a group of guards
He told you he was going

You screamed at your God
He invoked his God
You thanked your God
that you and she were not older and already
the father and mother of children
whom you would not have been able to save

Do we who are safe, when we see your image, recorded
as you stood in view of the cold little camera's eye,
think that human beings are like emptied sacks
that can simply be filled up again?

There may once have been a modest
        holiness in the small clearings in the woods
before they were land-mined
where the aid packages fell tangled in their parachutes
and were turned to bait for booby traps and ambush
Did modest holiness serve at least
        sometimes to hold back our predatory hands?

The person you are, or were, was used by others
Something you had was wanted by others
Something you are is hated by others
Maybe the way you hate who they are

Elsewhere, schoolhouses, warehouses, then the house of earth

The unthinkable has been buried by men driving bulldozers

Bus after bus arriving full, departing empty

We do not see what we see

WITH WINGS / CON ALAS

Versos de invierno para Hugo / Winter Lines for Hugo

We're in a bar, talking.
Riding a two-horse team
we jump from one to the
other: Spanish, English.
We switch mounts, ride two on
one, change gaits, and sometimes
we pull a wagonload
of what we would both say
and oppose saying.
                         While
we're talking I look at
snow falling through windows
behind you, but I think:
I can almost change that,
say "Montevideo,"
make myself feel I'm there—
when I go outside sun
will shine, the air will be
rich with scents of flowers
and burnt fuels: and as soon
as I think that, every
word that I say or you
say, that you hear or I
do, means something different
from what it meant when out
there it was freezing and
those were our winter lives
that we would return to
again after this warm
conversation. . . .
                         Does world,
nation, or neighborhood,
or the lone single life
we would describe, only

baffle our attempts, dwarf
our grasp and mute both tongues?
The body of words runs
under us and we try
to ride it gracefully.
Horses do stumble or
pitch a shoe, break their gaits,
pull against each other.
They're hardheaded as well
as beautiful; they balk.
We halt them and dismount:
that is, we are silent
a while. . . .

(Because we both know the
heft and hope, ice or heat,
of things and lives around
us that we could not dis-
believe, that became part
of us, we know that a
wall to which one couldn't
reliably point with
a word would be harder
by far to build; also
beyond any power to
tear down. Could a house or
a barricade be built
without a name for bricks?
Without exemplary
words it's not possible
to name heroes, villains,
to bless or curse, to chant
the good charm or recite
the sharp rhyme that hunts out
blame to condemn it or
whisper the promise that
might console or strike the
song-bells of wonder and

awe or lament all the
unfolding tragedies
or stand up to shout the
festivities of praise.)

　　. . . What did you say?
We were talking about
poems, books, about a team
of horses, but into
my head comes a vision
of Tom McGrath, who said,
"If I know anything
about poetry, then
Pegasus has wings all
right but it's a mule."
　　　　　　　　¡Un

mulo con alas! Tú
y yo, estamos en
un bar, parlando. . . .

St. Valentine's Eve

1

Here, it's not your particular virtues and beauty, great as they are, that I want
    to honor.
But simply that, like others before and after, whether for a week or a long life,
We have been lovers, have been in love.
So that after we are dead, our names may be—
If these words are read by anyone long after our time—
Reminding tokens of the rushing intensities that can seem to others
    familiarly, touchingly or irritatingly blind when lovers
Wander in quiet fantasies of how later years would be if lived together
And seize each other a little desperately not only because of desire but also
    because the gift is not to be refused.

In the dark winter quiet of early morning, in this quiet little house
While you are still sleeping, and in an unaccustomed bed because you are
    angry at me,
A faint train whistle arrives like a piece of striped candy
And I sit waiting for a chance, when you wake, to apologize, to reconcile us if
    I have the courage, and writing
For the future, so that someone may know in some far moment
Of our moment.

2

But when you woke and found me still here instead of gone to work we only
  argued our way somewhat further down the rift:
Your injury from my ways, my reactions, my faults; my protestation against the
  scale of your anger.
You say and I contest; I say and you contest.
Your injury, you feel, deep and true and too expectedly that of a woman at
  the hands of a man; mine small by comparison.
My injury, I feel, as true as yours, coming from your inability to live with
  flaws in me no worse than those I make way for in you.
Your reactions, you feel, long overdue and past patience; your reactions, I feel,
  overdetermined, explosive, extreme.
My reactions, I feel, patient and already bitten back for fear of provoking your
  hurt or anger; my reactions, you feel, on the contrary, cold and petty and
  sour and only seeking to humiliate or put down.
Your efforts at love and patience, you feel, great and tiring; mine, you feel,
  insufficient.
Failing to go any further toward the bottom of this rift, then, we leave each
  other's presence.

For some reason I do not know, in my cloisters there is some regent angle
Where conflict can often place me just as suddenly as a shift of lighting over a
  whole landscape when the sun is occluded and canyons fall into deep
  shadow;
At my worst, my recidivist cold and petty and sour and supercilious reactions
  that were warmed and enlarged and sweetened and even humbled by love
  of you and by your love, take their old angle of view again and see
  everything in their own bad light.
I have strained against my own formed nature to avoid that angle, to abstain
  from it, but I fail; and then I am seeing things as I would not wish to see
  them.
And to argue with you at all is, in terms of how we are and have been with
  each other, already to have lost you.

3

(And that I would write things down at all, no matter how freed from us
For the unforeseen shapes of the poem by this peculiar going away from
Oneself that writing words down is—that I would seem to reveal to strangers
What our private lives are truly like, whether in happiness or sorrow,
Is precisely one of my faults that you cannot accept, one to which you
Cannot reconcile yourself and how can I blame you.
The truth of this is sometimes cold and painful to me, as well. I could
Write as if for no one, only that, too, betrays—I could climb onto the
    shoulders of a poetry
Celebrating its little rites of recuperative soundings for some later remnant
And I could reach even higher to a shelf where poems can be put away,
Having been formed, having been brought by someone's obsessive attention
Toward the possibilities in the play of words that half chose themselves, the
    time-lapse film
Of words and sentences like ferns uncurling, tendrils reaching and grasping,
Meanings opening, blossoming, wilting, while rushing among them go rays of
    purpose like bees.)

4

I want to bring myself to say what's right.
I meet you in a hall of my own mind
And do not give you comfort as I should.
Then I hear you stir in the actual night.
But what might matter now, I don't say.
Perhaps you gave some hint that we could return
To one another by small steps, again.
Tonight, is that what I chose not to see?
By tact, as if our touch were accident,
We might discover what to do with arm
And leg, with hand and mouth, and all we've spoken
Would mean that lovers are the ones for whom
The difficulty of love makes love awaken,
Not those from whom it takes the will to mend.

5

Still dark outside and you are still sleeping
And I am thinking of saying to you that together, early,
Before the sun comes up,
Let's raise the shades and let it be the lucidity of our rooms
That falls first on the frozen ground outside;
Together let's rhyme woes with some future rose,
Together light candles for our dead and our living,
Together vituperate the mystificating morning paper and laugh at its feeble
    fawning.
(Let us recommend to the editor-in-chief that he fly a K-Mart to Kampala
    and give it all away, that he liberate all children from the minds of
    marketers.)
Together we will plan our small resistances against large orders
And a small salvaging from great disorder
And . . .
We will throw the bedclothes across the window sill into the cleansing cold of
    winter sun,
We will believe of the moon that it rose last night through the black up-
    reaching branches of the winter trees.

6

For the sake of the survival of a feeling that can't be sold

For the sake of the light of thought that slants across imaginary landscapes
And for the sake of the light of sun or lamp that lifts every lovely and sordid
    detail into view in the landscapes, townships, city streets, that are real

For the sake of the storm that blows wind from afar through the trees
For the sake of the trees that thrash in the storm and do not fall

For the sake of men using up their lives in the mere carrying of burdens while
    mules on their hind legs speak of what is right
For the sake of not throwing oneself off a height or away in an unwanted role

For the sake of the white-lit, bright-lit, white-signed, late-night corner cafe
    on an otherwise desolate corner of the metropolis
For the sake of small rainwater puddled in the wide street

For the sake of a hand with only three fingers, holding a tool or turning a
    page
For the sake of a book

For the sake of all those to be remembered

For the sake of a feathered moment
Ours, this mind-wide moment

From *Maybe It Was So* (1991)

The Affect of Elms

Across the narrow street from the old hotel that now
houses human damage temporarily—
deranged, debilitated, but up and around in their odd
postures, taking their meds, or maybe trading them—

is the little park, once a neighboring mansion's side yard,
where beautiful huge old elm trees, long in that place,
stand in a close group over the mown green lawn
watered and well kept by the city, their shapes expressive:

the affect of elms is of struggle upward and survival,
of strength—despite past grief (the bowed languorous arches)
and torment (limbs in the last stopped attitude of writhing)—

while under them wander the deformed and tentative
persons, accompanied by voices, counting their footsteps,
exhaling the very breath the trees breathe in.

A Rememberer

It's a long list of those who had
less than nothing, who borrowed the money
for bread, who heard instead of a melody
the wind that whistled in under the door
in the bad hour between last light and night,
who must await neither friend nor kin
but force from strangers.

You'd read by the window a while longer.
Or give it up and wrap
your shoulders in a blanket, try to doze
in the dusty chair out of the drafts,
too tired to read.
Even half-sleeping, you'd go over
the memorized lines, not needing more than a whisper
to bring them back, with no one listening.
So I think of you
guarding the words inside
till they could find their road
to the world, or worlds could change.

In a small blue patch of specific chill
you sit—in time,
in that year, on that night, breathing
through stillness and cold
those words that could fill the lungs with air
or a ship with buoyancy over the deep,
that could fill memory with sweetness and grief,
hopelessness with hope,
with life, the stubborn mind.

homage to Nadezhda Mandelstam

LONG-AGO YAUPON

after Eugenio Montale

To rest—hidden, midafternoon, lightheaded and hot
in the only shade, the hollow center of a yaupon bush
when the glare needled in and no one would come,
to wonder about snakes, and listen to the wasps;

to watch the red ants in a spread-out horde search
the cracked ground around you and underneath, so many
ant miles from the great city mounds you'd dynamited
with hoarded firecrackers and then seen them rebuild;

to peer out of the bush at the low flat roof of the house,
its crushed white gypsum driving the sunlight back
while the locusts, we called them, raised their buzz
to fits of screeching across the bare acres;

and carefully crawling out with empty lunch sack and water jar
at last, self-exiled from the house but who cared,
to wonder with a boy's beginnings of sadness if all life and the work of men
wouldn't require hiding from the scald of light
under a bush topped with the throbbing paper nest of hornets.

STARS

Her head bowed, the mother is silent now,
weak, with tears on her face; the father's
too weary to push his voice at the boy
any longer, and out of reasons why he should.

The boy, chin pointed at them both,
backs away another step, one hand behind him
reaching for the door he will close on them.
Everything is slowing now, running out, wearing down.

On the table the tepid food lies abandoned.
A cold breath across vast space goes
between them in this silence, and away
from each other they whirl in gigantic arcs.

Lovers

Here is how it can be between a man and a woman.

In this handkerchief of his are tears he cried today—
over her, for her, he doesn't know why he cried—
when she smiled a little, when he saw her
recover, a little, from her fragility,
when he thought how much he loved her;
how desperately he hoped she would be happy.

Once, she gave him a handkerchief of hers, perfumed
in the instant when, standing before him alone,
she pushed it down into her panties and pressed it
against herself and brought it out again
still neatly folded, and smiling she gave it to him
to carry with him on his journey.

Mischief, happiness, sorrow, desire.

HARK

Stars in the clear night sky more silent than any other silence,
even a cave's; and yet at each star the noise of fusion
blasts to beggar rockets massed in the millions, a roaring
multiplied to futile infinity out there, in the soundless sky
over us, as we lie close listening to each other breathe,
hearing each other's heartbeats, sensing the smallest
candlewick of each other's noiseless warming desire.

Poem

Early on, uncertain, when we had
those few stolen clouded days along
a cold shore, in a gloomy house
an angle of sunlight shone in
for a moment and warmed us.

But with you for our secret while
that afternoon I lost my voice; I was
bewildered by you, made other by you,
and couldn't make, for that hour,
any sound at all, much less speak.

Now it seems to me I had to change
to become who I needed to be to be with you.
Now it seems to me that I needed to begin
over again from a time before I could speak.
Now it seems to me it was also through you
that then words came back to me.
Maybe it was so I could love you.
Maybe it was so I could say to you that I love you.
Maybe it was so I could say what I meant, to anyone.

From a Paper Boat

White gulls are brightest against the green river.
Flowers quicken, their hues flame, against the blue hill.
Just when I look, spring is over, once more.
When, on what day, will I be able to go home?
—Tu Fu

The Emperor awarded me a year's living.
I spent the first two months in a mountain temple.
The blue trees at dusk were full of crows.
Then in early spring I traveled to visit friends.

At night cold mists would gather, covering the stars.
To most of my friends life seemed endless war.
No one desired leisure for thought, but only to keep busy.
It snowed a little each night, and each day the sun melted the snow.

~

I had wished to spend time thinking and observing alone.
Departing without fanfare, as if again on the Emperor's business,
I had chosen to leave behind all responsibilities.
But soon I missed my family and decided I would return to them.

Then came the night of calamity darker than ten thousand nights.
Events cut me off, and when finally I reached our city
It had been destroyed, and with it all traces of my heart's care.
I repaired a small abandoned boat, and set out on the river.

~

Slowly I drifted away from our city, it did not matter to me where.
The riverbanks were scorched, and beyond them on both sides
Lay buildings blown down in the ashen streets.

I saw one burnt uncanny hand sticking up
Stiffly from a mere shadow, and remains
Of houses, crushed and tilted and collapsed
As if they had been no more than folded paper.

~

In my wandering, after all whom I had loved
Were lost, at first I chose familiar harbors
So as to see the friends of my earlier years
From whose warm houses my itinerant service

Had always returned me to my own house, in time.
After mooring with haste to a quay of stone
I would leave my boat with quickened step
To find the streets and friends I remembered.

We would drink wine and talk all night long.
But now I tie up carefully and stay ashore only a short time.
I do not wish to see anyone I know. I buy my provisions,
I draw clean water from the town fountain, I return to my boat alone.

We used to sit outside among orange blossoms and jasmine
In the candlelit dark. But our talk made me feel unclean:
Each of us with his own complaint, mine not always the worst;
Or recounting, sometimes beautifully, the stories of victims.

~

Several times, in my years of service, I had had to move my family.
Mostly we lived far from the capital cities, in smaller towns.
Each day I was happy to return home from the fruitlessness of offices.
When I saw my wife come out to meet me, crossing the muddy cobbles,
Her every step endeared her to me.

Three times she made another being out of herself.
Once she wept over a dead child, no larger than her own hand.

Twice, with the blessings of gods and spirits, she gave birth to a son.
She was more precious to me than all the Emperor's jade.
Yet when my year of leisure was awarded to me, I chose to travel away.

∼

The villages along the riverbank, for all their differences,
Their raids and rivalries, will always lie under the same stars;
And despite the changes in me and in this river,
When I lie on my back at night and look up,
My memories are the same, they can see me no matter where I go.

∼

I remember the night when, in the small hours,
Having eluded muggers on the train platforms
And along the dark lengths of city blocks,
I returned home in the deep shadows.

After treading quietly up the steps of my porch,
At the door I hesitated with my key.
My family was asleep inside, safely sheltered.
But I had brought with me the echoes of danger.

∼

Once I heard someone say angrily behind me, "Hurry up!"
When I turned I saw middle-aged men and women crossing the street.
They had fat cheeks, small eyes, open mouths, a slow gait.
They were held back in dulled childhood by the accidents they had inherited.
I went home early, and my sons came running to greet me.

∼

When we lived in the north, my wife and I rose early in summer.
We took our tea out to our back step, and sat down there.
Over us and our small house stood a great willow tree.

Filled with a choir of birds, it seemed a protecting spirit.
She sat with her back straight, and looked into my eyes.

Then in under–a–blanket weather when horses ran at dawn
And at night the clear sky strewed galactic lilies
Far beyond and above the rushing of the cold earthly wind,
Inside and in silence we drank tea together by the fire,
Our heads close, knowing each other's thoughts.

~

Columns of boy conscripts still move over the roads.
Sometimes I have had to float past their riverbank camps at night,
With rags wrapped around my oar, to avoid their questions and threat.
They are always wearing new uniforms and boots,
And carrying new guns, new radios, new missiles, old swords.

~

I wonder what our sons would have remembered of their childhood.
I recall what I would wish to forget.
There is almost nothing that does not come back to me.
Memory strikes my legs and gives me an idiot's gait of grief.
Any child's presence returns me to my longing for my own.

~

I remember walking on Washington Street in my native city,
I heard, "Shut up!" I turned and saw a sobbing three–year–old
Being hauled down the sidewalk by one arm, too fast.
I thought of taking ripe plums from a tree, and finding them bitter.

~

That my sons would marry someday made me study young women.
I saw that some put themselves frighteningly at mercy:
In any café or gathering, the one whose lips held a cigarette

That a man's bullwhip would flick out; and the one
Around whom a knife-thrower was carefully patterning his daggers;
The one thrown repeatedly into the air who kept turning
Graceful somersaults as she fell back; and the one
Lifted in the lead elephant's mouth. To all these,
The great crowd roared its happiness at seeing them so endangered.

~

I was in the aisle of a supermarket one afternoon.
I heard behind me, "Put that back! Stop, damn it!"
I did not turn—I heard a smack, and the sort of small crying
That is already guarded, holding itself in.

~

That memorable night when I returned home late, I hesitated.
I stood in front of my door chasing a thought I never caught.
Finally I put my key in the lock, and went in.
After I had shut the door behind me, I stood alone.

Only one lamp was burning in the quiet house.
I said, Hurry up! Shut up! Stop, damn it! to the floor, to myself.
It was to test the power of demons that I spoke those things.
But that night my family was asleep and safe.

~

I have breathed again the scent of my children's rumpled beds.
I have received a hundred times the fateful letter from the Emperor.
Ten thousand times I have missed my chance to look into my wife's eyes
With thankfulness to her before we were never to see each other again.

~

Like stars in a small constellation that follow a brighter star,
Like a string of skiffs tied behind a slow-sailing ship,

Like cribs in a row down an orphanage ward,
Like goslings in a line behind a goose,
A file of small children walking along, I remember.

They were beside the green lawn of a saint's church, making no sound,
Each one reaching forward and back to hold the hands of others.
I thought they had been inside to see the mythical frescoes.
But they were led strictly by a nun, they were all blind.
They were out for the air, for the movement of their hesitant legs.

~

In the headlights of my stopped car on an empty country road,
My two small sons were chattering to each other, their hands darting.
It was after heavy rain, when the ditches were hissing.

Another car might come along, and I called to them.
Ten thousand new frogs no bigger than little grapes
Were hopping in the road, and my boys wanted to save them.

~

In a seaside town all of one color stone it was torrid summer.
For a week my wife and I rented a bedroom whose rightful tenant,
A widow, moved into her kitchen for the money we paid her.
In the morning we swam, in the afternoon we returned to the town.

Inside the hot shuttered bedroom we made love. Then we slept,
Breathing the sea-washed scent of our arms, our tangled legs.
When we woke it was cool again, and we went out, looking at each other.
We walked along the top of the high town walls, beside the sea.

~

I am told of armies of orphan soldiers marching and destroying.
Once, I saw a band of big ragged boys—that might have been them.
They walked slowly in the heat, laden with dusty weapons.
One of them led a young woman by a rope tied around her neck.

Sometimes, visiting an old friend, surprising him
With my coming unannounced when he had thought me dead,
I was greeted with happiness and a few oranges.
Then I heard of what one army or the other had done.

～

Many women admire the male strength that is not used
Against them. Or rather, when the male strength
Is restrained, holding its own arms back, force acting
With a volunteered tenderness, then many women admire it.

～

I have often seen young girls playing,
Unaware of what adults knew. They gambol through
The shopping malls and city streets pulling at
Their tired silent fathers who come bored and afraid
And angry from work in factories and mines.

Who come wanting to protect their beloved daughters.
If it were a daughter of my own listening to me
I would not want her to hear of what I have seen.
But when telling, why do I wish to tell
Of the end of hope, of the prison of what is?

～

When I watched my sons play, I always hoped
That there was neither evil of which I did not know
Already stalking them, nor any suffering
Nor any distortion of their small being that I myself
Might inflict on them. I wanted to hide them away,
As if they were gold coins never to be spent.

I did not want their lives to fail of my witness.
As soon as I was apart from my sons, even for an hour,
I felt a terrible urgency to hurry back to them.

I was afraid for their safety. I could scarcely think.
Yet, even loving them as I did, when they were around me
I might chase them off so that I could continue my thinking in peace.

~

As a child, my wife was hardly noticed.
Her father was an important man; her mother followed his wants.
I never remembered my own childhood very clearly.
My wife said it had fallen into a chasm of shadow
So that I might not suffer from having to see it again.

~

When our children were small, at night my wife's legs ached.
From standing and bending and carrying, she suffered pain.
I would invite her to sit calmly, take out her hairpins, rest.

I massaged the graceful length of her legs.
I brought a bowl of warm water for her sacred feet.
I washed them and rubbed warmth into her papery skin.

Thus also I cleansed my stale soul, my hands, of tobacco and ink.
I hoped then, I hope now, she did not dislike me.
From her came the fragrance of vanilla and scalded milk, of patience.

~

Sometimes I tie up beside a noisy riverman's hut full of life.
When a large boat passes, its wake reaches to each shore.
The wake does not move the hut or the banks of the river,
But it beats against my skiff, rocking me in it.

After the riverman's family is asleep,
The moon silvers the rippling wake of each night-sailing boat.
From on board, the sound of a man and woman talking
Will travel across the water, unknown to them.

It seems to me then that they are in life and I am no longer.
I grow older but I can grow no older.
They are traveling toward life, they look ahead to glimpse
And guess at it. I see it clearly, receding behind me.

~

In almost every man and woman I have met, I mark the child—
In the demeanor and gestures, in the way of smiling and of weeping,
In the casual greeting, whether it is open or guarded,
In the manner of defeat and in the moment of contentment.
Do others mark a child in me?
Is it too late to welcome the boy within the stringent man?
Is it too late to give refuge to the girl within the mirrored woman?
The wars of childhood come to an end,
But everyone who survives remains a refugee.

~

Students stood thick in the square like grain before harvest.
After childhood, before manhood, there is a time
Of being only half in life. The other half
Stands not in death but in illusion and courage.
The full moon was following a red star
Through the sky each night, unable to catch it.

I was there, in the capital city. My boat was hidden
Under a ruined bridge where no lost people slept.
At one end of the immense square, soldiers shouted
Through trumpets and raised a huge flag.
At the other, defiant students in their faded caps
Stood thick as the grain before the harvest.

~

Now is a time of endings—of the year, the decade, the century.
Now opposites will struggle with more ferocity.

At night a gull looks black; the river is falling.
After midnight I am often startled by sirens and gunshots.

I lie awake in my boat, looking up and listening.
The Milky Way glows like spilled jewels too numerous to be gathered again.
From ten thousand houses I hear crying and shouts of despair.
Softer, some nights, there is laughter and a little singing.

Sometimes I can return to sleep. Sometimes I light
A candle and take out paper. I dip my brush in ink
And write out poems that I remember. Lines written down
In solitude survive, and I am in them as I write them.

～

All day geese cross the autumn sky, calling to each other.
Then a yellow moon rises, prodigious beyond masts and rooftops.
Late in the night, I hear more geese overhead.
Their voices come down as if from another time.

The limbs of my children were delicate, their speaking precise.
In autumn I sat one night under the sky, listening for geese.
I remember my older son coming up behind me, I heard him approach,
He put his small hand on my shoulder and said, "Papa?"

My heart lies nearly still inside my ribs.
I remember his voice and that touch, and his childish handwriting.
I cannot think why I should breathe
Unless it were to hear the geese once more.

～

Yet it must be love, and even the memory of love,
Which, like clear water from a blue pitcher,
Spills over one's naked shoulders and hips
And rinses grief from the body,
Splashing it to the thirsty ground.

~

But my river has arrived at a place of sand where it is swallowed up.
I must walk across mountains and a dry plain.
Walking is a different rhythm from rowing or tending my sail:
My thoughts will wander with me in a different way.

I will keep my provisions, my brush and inkstone in a doll's house.
I will carry the doll's house on my back till I reach water again.
I will step out of my boat and turn and pick it up, too,
Carefully I will fold it and put it into my pocket.

I look back. Bright gulls are whitest against the river's green.
Against the blue hill flowers flame, their hues quicken.
Just when I look, spring is over, again.
On what day will I be able to go home? When?

AN EXPLOSION

It isn't the way it was
when he had strong legs,
thick arms, a handsome
wide back, and, in his house
clothes—rolled-up shirt
sleeves and a soft baggy
pair of pants that he especially
enjoyed putting on
after bathing—he would roam out
exhausted and loose-limbed
calling the three small boys
in for supper, and laughing
would gather them all at one time
and hold them hard against
his veiny body till they squirmed
and in that way he worked free
of his long shift in the pit.
At such moments he was kinder
than he was, and his wife, alive
and young then, seeing him
with his sons, could not but excuse
his other moments, and allow him
and everyone their choices,
although she would not
forgive the eternal owners
of the hollow hill.

He would trade the scrap of life
that he still has, but where
is the taker? His thin arms hang
and his neck's frail, his step's
cautious, he's cold, he coughs
and stands with others among whom
no one happens to know him
anymore near the mouth of the mine.

Several souls silently
rocket up unnoticed by anyone,
launched from inside the earth
and spinning like starfish thrown
as far out into the deep
earth's shadow as any
god's arm could fling them.

And a camera crew pushes hot
repelling lights and a mike
at the old man's face, which says,
"I've been waiting all night
for my babes, I'm
hoping that they are alive."

MADRID

Through stone portals and under colonnades
into the old central plaza in cold December
came gypsies and outcasts with green branches.

They had broken off boughs of pine and spruce
along their minor routes to the city.
They had stripped copses and groves and plantations.

They camped on the cobbles, they lived in tents and wagons.
They sold the branches and a few small trees; some begged.
Little fires flickered in their artificial forest.

They seemed to have brought with them into the plaza
the stillness they had torn out of the woods,
as if to sustain the peace that the city would tear out of them.

Overheard, their voices sounded raw and smoky, used up.
But late, rising above the noise of cars and of children
playing at all hours, there might be a guitar and singing.

Catching my coat sleeve, their beautiful dirty children
improvised intricacies of delay, so as to praise and hawk
the scent of green, so as to implore and beguile.

I was outside their thoughts, I was outside their ways.
We judged each other, I bought the wasted pine boughs.
The children stole my coin, I stole their image.
Now we are all outside that time, we are all inside this language.

HIDE FROM TIME

for wife and daughter

I was about to return to our Sunday,
love, to the two of you, but a sliver of winter
sunlight lay on the stair like a feather.

Rather than mountains or any beautiful
view of mountains, rather than rivers
down which I could float my gaze,

I'd want this stray feather on the stairs
up to our room and our daughter's room
far from airplanes and faraway hurricanes

of night-fears and the daily inevitable
beginnings of the workdays schooldays
when she leaves and I leave and you leave

pulling threads of each other with us
through the hours while the luckless must seek
shelter and warmth and the loveless

must hope and connive and believers
must pray and depressives must live
their un-life unwillingly

and we hope we won't, our daughter will never,
be one of those, at the mercy of others, of all
that changes, of hard everything, iron and ironic.

This isn't a feather I can pick up.
It's starting to fade—a cloud or the movement
in one minute of the earth. *Are you coming?*

you call to me. This universe is still creating itself
and like all mere life maybe we come from
four billion years ago till we three

spin into being and braid our courses.
From the decks of ships I've seen what infinity
looks like in the night sky, it pulls vision

away, far past the intervening mist
of stars, until for all their known size
they seem only trembling microbes of light

in the biggest dish, and as if we've been
tossed up by a wave from the incalculably
slow churning, microbes on a microbe,

electrons on an atom of an atom,
we float in mid-cosmos,
life an instant, before we fall back

alongside but faster than
flensed planets and ipsitive suns,
all the most and least promising things.

Now I'm going, too. I call, *I'm coming.*
The feather's gone and you're waiting.
Both of you, I love.

TEACHER

Stillness and silence deepen in the last light.

Across the glossy luminous water a muskrat
noses a passage, trailing a clean wake.
Nearer, circles ripple outward where a fish
came up with open jaws on a mayfly.

The fire crumbles down, crackling.
Near the canoe, the washed skillet and plates
drip upside down onto a cold rock-shelf.

The wind begins to breathe and blow
through the spruce-tops, they creak and the food duffel
sways where we hung it, up in the branches, high.

At this little lake, this floor
of one shaft of heaven, the peppermint
we trampled when we were hammering stakes
scents our darkness inside the tent;
mosquitoes patter against the nylon like rain.

We shift and settle our hips and shoulders
till they'll accept their own weight. It's only
a little, what we know or hope to know.

The loons seem to break their laughter with a cry.

From *Saints* (1986)

EATING

As if it's been waiting until he can't have it,
some moment they lived, that he didn't want
when it was his, begins to raise a craving in him—
good dinner that she used to hear him
bring thoughtfully upstairs to where
she was waiting—reading or watching TV.
They'd spend a half-hour eating it,
their familiar life was a comfort, then from
the next room where he'd be brooding
over books or just hoarding himself
he'd listen for her quiet movement,
sometimes laughter as she watched TV or read.
Did she want him to think she was happy?
But he'd sit still and ponder what
was expected of him, or hoped.
Later they'd snack, or one of them would.

Remorse now makes him remember her saying
one time when they were crying in her new
living room filled with familiar things
that were just hers, not his anymore,
"I wish I'd stayed to have breakfast with you."
She meant all those mornings she had
hurried away to work, him still in bed
debating with himself whether to get up,
whether to have an egg or skip to lunch.

(Once at a dinner when they were admiring
all the work their hosts had finished together
on floors and walls, but famished, she had
told him how she liked something he had done
and he'd bitten at her, red with his own
unsuspected anger, then sick at her tears.)

It wasn't her fault he'd lain in bed.
His too-wistful asking her to stay those mornings

only showed he thought it would be easier
if she went, though there were days
he'd get up to walk to the diner
with her at that special pace they hit
together, that came to life from them
like a child, but was broken
when after breakfast he watched her go on
alone to work and he walked the other way,
full of coffee and bread—

As it would break if they were tired
after those dinners with friends
when they'd eaten too much. And even if
he'd done nothing cruel, walking home
side by side late and out of step,
each could silently take back—
and he often would—what had seemed
affectionately given in the company of others.
A brief safe walk to bed—the distance
sometimes growing, the closer they got to home.
And in bed, whether they did or they didn't;
snugged against each other or not;
with the silence denying all hurts
or tears from either or both;
with him refusing to answer
or her taking a sharp
quick breath to say *yes;*
good food and too much wine
or bad and none—

                    they were hungry
lying awake, and hungry they fell asleep,
and sleeping, all night long, they were hungry.

ELSEWHERE CHILDREN

In the icy block between Madison and Monroe
walking slowly and unbalanced
by the two unequal bags of layers of
bags of apparently nothing

she who was once somebody's darling—
and the somebody lost to her years
ago and forgotten, maybe, along with birthdays
and beatings and other things that were best

forgotten—has stopped in a doorway.
Two persons come walking by her unaware,
a young woman who is saying "There's *something*
I need, not sure what," and a young man

with goatee and thin dirty gloves
who answers, "You looking for a man to protect you!"
This woman he's been wishing for and has
just met frowns and slows down;

with her "I'm all right" they stop near
the old one's shallow niche out of the wind.
(What cold hand turned her this way? When?
Last year? Or the year she was four

or five, so long ago?) The young woman
stamps her cheap sleek boots in the salty slush
and splashes the man's wet running shoes,
she says, "I'm hungry" and he answers, hoping

maybe coffee will be enough for her, "My son says
Daddy you going to eat eggs this morning?—
I say no more, man, not no more! I heard they
really bad for you!" And he laughs down at the shoes

so useless to him, at the wonder of a world
beyond his powers. The old woman squints up at him
but the young one with him only says,
looking off, "My little girl's seven."

Separate parents, she and he, of elsewhere children.
(Where did the old woman's father leave her
one day, the start of the path here,
if just with a way of saying no or yes?)

My own dearborn, away from me today,
with secrets already of puzzling
not quite thinkable harm
(I know, because at my slight warnings

sometimes inside you a troubling echo
I can't hear alarms you, you say
"Don't tell me that or I'll worry
about it all night and I won't be able to sleep!")—

my only-five-years-old, with a soul
already taught by pain to be articulate
and beginning already to wrinkle, let no day
or disappointment ever turn you

toward a street as cold and hungry as this.
Let someone show me please how to keep
you from it if I can, if they can.
As for wishing you always free of ordinary pain,

like a father's or a mother's, I might
as well wish food into dead refrigerators
and the warmth to come out of these store-windows
into the street and do some good.

Then the young woman and man walk away.
And she who was once somebody's darling

blinks them away and gone in the between-buildings light,
they could be her children, she was once

someone's, but she can't look after them,
we can't look after our own.

MAKE ME HEAR YOU

When my Aunt Lera—tiny now,
slow moving and slow talking—
wanted to tell me about
her life, she began by saying
"Curtis and me had just one . . .
year . . . together." Curdiss
(the way she says it) was
a genial great man by all
remembrances of him, and the two
of them, just married, would go
fishing in the evening from
the banks of the Pearl,
the green stream in Mt. Olive,
Mississippi. A year of that—
quiet aloneness together
after supper, I imagine,
and the things each showed
the other, and the bed turned down—
but then Curdiss's father
came to live with them
in their tiny house and while
Curdiss was away at work
in the mill the old man would
find his way out to the yard
and have fits, twirling around,
falling, so she'd have to
pick him up and carry him
back inside, and that was
how they lived till
all too soon Curdiss
died, and then his father.

Dead Curdiss is Lera's
old ghost who has flown with her
into every day, the lost chance
to live alone with him as he was

and could have been, and you're
a ghost who'll fly alongside
me into the ruins and rooms
I was the one who decided
we would never share
again—you'll hover up just
when you see the thing you want
to show me, and unable to
make me hear you, unable to hear
me say back to you, *Oh love, I would
never have seen that without you.*

for V.

Two Kinds of Singing

1 After Salvador Díaz Mirón's "Example" (1901)

The public corpse was rotting on the branch
like hideous fruit that drooped against the stem;
the proof of an improbable decree,
it swayed above the road like a pendulum.

The shameless nakedness, the bulging tongue,
a shock of hair straight up like a rooster's comb—
it had the look of farce; and a ragged gang
of boys, all jokes, stood grinning by my horse.

And the mournful sack of guts, with head bowed down,
swollen outrage on the green hanging tree,
vented a putrid stench in the strong gusts
as like a censer in solemn arcs it swung.
And the sun was rising through a flawless blue:
Tibullus put such landscape into song.

2   After Osip Mandelstam's #54 (1913)

Bread that's poisoned, and not a sip of air,
how hard it is to get a wound to heal.
Joseph himself, sold to Egypt to slave,
could not have been more heavily grieved.

But under starry skies the Bedouins come,
they still their horses, and with eyes closed
invent a story—a rambling epic poem
of the vague day they've lived through, almost bored.

Among them, little's needed to inspire—
who lost a quiver in the sand,
how a trade of geldings went—events
are a mist that starts to thin and disappear.

And if the song is sung out to the end,
wholeheartedly, with all the breath in the lungs,
everything vanishes—and what remains
is the vast space, the stars, the one who sings.

HER LOVE

A man whose son has died has
to forgive the boys who
still live, when they come
up the street slowly in
a ragged group, talking, three
with mitts, one with the ball.
Should forgive, and does.
Because whatever first trust there was
in anything is gone now, anyway,

and what he could never think
of losing has been lost.
But the woman he loves
says we are not cups to be poured empty
and there's no measure in being mad.
So when she offers him what
she has, her love, he takes it
greedily, thankfully, glad.

THAT PHONE CALL

You were saying the radio that cold morning
had come on early, but with birdsong,
the dawn chorus, people call it

(while here the silent chill was falling
over my bed from the warped window as I still slept—
still dim here, lighter where you were).

Summer songs in the stiff morning!
You'd waked Katie and said, Listen.
And you'd cried at being alive and healing

while new tumors had come up, you'd heard,
beneath your loved friend's papery scars.
The day got worse (that waiting, then, was bad;

things we couldn't resolve were holding
the peace we wanted away from us like a handful
of medicine we felt we had to have)

but the sun shone for a while, you said,
cars came and went on the icy road.
I listened, I could see your shoulders,

the kitchen fluorescence like black-and-white
over you and the letters and the cigarettes
and cold coffee cup by the telephone.

I'm down, you said, I'm tired, I'm blue
again, help me get to sleep.
I could see your black hair, your mouth,

your legs inside your warm robe.
I couldn't help seeing them!
It was dark here when we spoke, darker there.

We couldn't harmonize on "she'll
be comin' round the mountain when
she comes" for Kate's delight, or sit

still talking to each other after
her bedtime, or, coming closer, touch.
What you would be able to do for your friend

was going to be hard and it wouldn't save her.
It's no use, you said. I'll hang up.
Don't, I said. Wait a little longer.

And the bridge of an old love song
I'd been trying for days to remember
came to me then, tightening my throat

around the tune as if I'd never
lost it or worried I'd forget, and I said,
Sing this song to me, it's not

too soon for you to start singing
us all awake, let song carry
the blue away till we can be together,

wait, I'm listening, sing—
you sing it and I'll sing, too.

APRIL TO MAY

Innumerable fresh starts of which
nothing or little needs to be made
have built a heap of possibilities
for me, for nearly anyone,
since a day two weeks ago
that marked the death of a friend.
It's too soon to be surprised
to see the paper scrap still
pinned above desk and letters and photos—
name and telephone number
of this woman who has died.

It would be a comfort,
almost, to have followed—instead
of her slow decline that made her
lurch and trip along the path
the rest of us miraculously walked—
the surprising inevitable fall
of a good sad story in which
the troublesome colt is finally
shot by a passing soldier, or the heroine's
left to die—she insists
that the others go on—
by the river in flood.

But what happened to our friend
was not a good story, nothing
in the sad ending's right.
Or rather, she and her suffering
ended and the story didn't
stop for her. Everywhere
alphabets are all still
in use, small children easily
speak what foreigners won't master
with the years of practice to come,
there are acts and letters of new

apostles, the struggles against them
continue. It's raining today.
Lice and azaleas and racehorses
are flourishing. The May light's
lengthening into the nights
she no longer sleeps in.

Her attempts and hopes, the air
in her rooms that lifted
her scent to me when she passed,
and her voice—nothing of her
is moving with the fast current,
everything of her drifts to a stillness,
left in an eddy with all
that's finished, a dry leaf
on the water, deepening,
while every real living
one of us has rushed a little
farther these few minutes,
afloat with our grief and opportunity,
still calling back—

hours of her, days,
               April to May.

Away from You

Sounds of crickets and chickadees
A wasp crawling on the inside of the porch screen
Plaintive small whistle of a white-crowned sparrow
Morning cicadas in the trees by the hot garden
I think of holding gently a tight fistful of your
       black hair and kissing you
A house chair left outside in the sun near the tomatoes
You stood me before the doors I'd kept closed
A jay honking and lecturing, won't stop,
       in the cedars—like me
A huge black ant wobbling by as it carries another
You have been the way that was opened for me
Motionless planks slanted against the cabin-side
       and an empty tin bucket under them
Against you I've limped till I could walk again
       and then beside you walked
Till hurt and limping; and stayed, even when
       you did the hurting
Whatever wildflower blossom you are, I'm still
       not sure of your name
Weathered wood, new blooms, quiet peace,
       leaning tree, the open cabin door
Everything, when I am in my thoughts of you,
       begins to signify
I want to be, I want to have been
       what you have been for me
For you

For C.

SAINTS

All violent people secretly desire to be
curbed by something that they respect,
so that they become known to themselves.
—Allen Tate

O that thou shouldst give dust a tongue
        To cry to thee
    And then not hear it crying!
—George Herbert

1 The Blue Dress

You tore it off my back.

But I'm not good
at telling a story—you'd shut
me up by saying that—
so I guess I can't tell this one,
that has to do with the way
I once used to feel
when someone like you
who had done a rough kind
of work—work that can kill you
if you're not careful—talked
to me like my listening
was important to him.
                And listened
to me, too, made me feel
I could be the gentleness
he needed after bad
times—someone who'd grown
up hard and alone, like you,
or gotten through the war
alive. . . . But I don't feel
the same about you any

more, or nearly anyone,
any man, I've known.
I thought when I met you
and it was exciting to me
to be with you, it was
more life I was getting—
and it was less.

But you said I was special,
I was the best of all
the girls—the women—you'd had,
the sexiest, I turned you on
the most. That's what I'd
remember when I'd want
to leave you, when you'd been
after me again, like always,
drunk, hunting me or saying
you'd kill me. I'd try remembering
that nobody else ever told me
I was special or beautiful,
and I thought it was loving
me that made you say it—
I know I'm not pretty
the way some women are,
the way some were that you
would look at twice and make
me forget what you'd done
and want you for myself again.

But it was just being
scared that kept me from leaving,
you saw to that many times.
And I did used to love you,
I did love your kisses,
love that touch you had for me,
holding my face in your hands,
squeezing my shoulders for me,

the way you'd rub my tired legs
and how you'd put your hands
on my breasts, that was so careful,
I thought, not to hurt.
And my gripping you as hard
to me as I could, and you'd
say I was the best of all
of them, the best and the best
till the waves of it hit—
I'd float for a long
second or two and then it
slams through, so sweet.

But you'd hit me. Just sitting
together in the apartment and you'd
jump up and hit me yelling
"Don't do that!" and I don't
even know what it is.
You used your belt on me,
you threw me down the stairs
more than once and locked
me out alone for hours
and I never knew anyone
in the building who I could
go to, I'd just stay down
near the front door inside,
people would come in and go out
and hold the door for me
but I'd say no, I was
waiting for someone. . . .

Till you came down to look.
When you made up to me
I was so happy to have
you back—back to yourself—
and we'd go out dancing,
you'd know everybody there

and those friends of yours would always
pretend that nothing's wrong.
I felt grateful to them
for treating me so friendly,
so polite, so respectful. Nice.
And they could laugh with me,
in a way you couldn't, or wouldn't.

The preacher says to talk.
So I do and he listens
and doesn't say very much.
He still thinks that all
the bad came from you, that
everything bad that was done,
you did—which I'm not going
to tell him any different.
All he knows about that
night is you chased me
downstairs and into the street
at 3 A.M. with me
in my nightgown in the cold and no shoes
and you with the sharp kitchen
knife in your hand, yelling
you were going to cut me.

You never even knew how
afraid I was to go
to sleep and afraid to wait up
for you, too, but what would
you have cared, in those moods—
I went crazy wondering
what you'd do when you came in,
turning like a mean dog
and trying to get me when you
could barely stand up and had
to hold onto the furniture
to walk across the room.

I don't know how you
were able all of a sudden
to move so fast that night,
the state you were in, and the knife
in your hand. Then when you stopped
in the middle of the dead
street and said it was over
and turned around and started
back, I don't know why
I followed you home, either.

I watched you real carefully
when you got into bed
with your clothes on and you put
the knife under your pillow
and said to me that if I
wanted to kill you while you
were sleeping, there it was.

I waited one more hour,
watching the clock go slow,
afraid you'd wake up
sick out of your alcohol sleep
and with one of your nightmares.
Then I had to reach under
your pillow to find the knife
and I cut my finger on it—
I almost cried out
but I realized that what I was
was so mad at you that
all of a sudden I wanted
to beat you hard as I could
with my fists and scream and it
still makes me crazy and I
wish I had done it—
instead. But I didn't
make a sound, just held

my cut finger that I couldn't
look at and looked at you
for a long time, trying
to guess where in you was your heart.

I had a thought and I
went back to the kitchen to put
a bandage on my cut and hold
it till it stopped bleeding
and only throbbed and I called
the police. Come over here
right now, I told them, I'm
going to kill him, and I gave
the address, the apartment,
the floor, the bedroom. . . . I wanted
a bunch of them in case
they had to save me from
what you might do while you
were dying.
                    Or maybe what
I wanted was what they did.

I took the knife and went
first to unlock the door
for when they'd come, wondering
how long it would be. I stood
in the doorway to our room
counting to two hundred
in my mind and then counted
again, and heard them stamping
and running up the stairs
so loud I thought they'd wake you
and I ran to stab your chest
holding the knife with both hands.

It slipped sideways and tore
your shirt down your ribs

and only cut you some.
You jumped and opened your eyes
but it didn't seem like you
could see me and I stabbed you
again and it slipped again,
I couldn't make it go
into you, but too late to stop.

When the cops pulled you off
of me—I don't know where
the knife went—know what?
I had to run onto the back
landing outside and pull
the door shut, that always
locks, lock myself out
because you were yelling
Help me, Esther, help me
please God Esther, help,
they're killing me, Esther!
I would have gone back
and killed those cops to get
them off of you.

Then the noise was gone away.
I was trying to figure out
how to get back in, freezing
and crying in my nightgown,
they must have taken you away
and what would happen to you
and how could I get you out
somehow when I heard two shots
from the street around front.
I don't know what they've said
you did—when they came up
calling for me and let me
into our place and told me
what had happened to you
I couldn't seem to hear them.

What I thought of while they
were talking and talking and waiting
for me to say something
that I wasn't going to say
was how I'd last seen one
of them at your back holding
you by the collar the way
you grabbed mine the night
you tore my new blue dress
that you couldn't tell from silk
right off my back, left me
naked in a corner with my hands
up and you yelling at me
I spent too much of your money,
said I wouldn't leave you alone,
made me get in the closet
and locked me in there, shouted
through the door if I ever
tried to leave you you would
cut me so bad, no one
would want me, while I cried
into a torn rag of my dress,
all ruined and lost and wasted.

That was for you, that dress,
to make you happy, make
you want to be with me.
All I had was a physical
need in my body, for you,
and wanting you to say
you loved me and be nice
the way you used to be.
I kept thinking that if
I was nicer to you
you'd get better, you'd be
all right again, and I'd
be special to you, like before.
Now nothing can change ever

between us, we'll always
be stuck where we were that night.
Only I'm the only one
to feel it, you can't.

The preacher will tell me I
should forgive you now,
should let it go, should come
to church once in a while,
I look at him and see
another man looking at me.
You used to tell all your
stories to your friends, the hard
knocks you'd had—you said
harder than mine. Is this
story good enough, you think,
for me to tell it? But you
aren't listening, you can't
answer me, you never did,
you're not here but you won't
go away, and you can't
give me back what you took
if you're dead. If you could
give me back that one dress
then you could give me everything,
even the way one time you put
your hand in my hair after
you had hit me and said
Please don't cry, sugar, don't,
honey, stop crying, please,
I promise to you that
I'll never do it ever again.

2 A Personal Need

Someone is worrying me and troubling my mind,
          bring me the mail

DO NOT OPEN THIS "CONFIDENTIAL MAIL"
UNLESS YOU LIVE AT THIS ADDRESS

DEAR FRIENDS IN CHRIST I'VE READ IT IN THE BIBLE
I RE-READ IT AND I PRAYED ABOUT IT AND I'VE HEARD
THE VOICE OF THE LORD SPEAKING TO MY HEART CONCERNING
YOU AND A NEED THAT YOU HAVE IN YOUR LIFE
I SAID "LORD OVER THE YEARS YOU HAVE SENT
DIFFERENT PEOPLE TO ME I KNOW YOU DID
AND LORD I'M PRAYING THAT YOU WILL SEND "THIS FAMILY"
THE SAME TYPE OF BLESSING THAT YOU DID
FOR OUR DEAR BROTHER RAYMOND WHEN HE NEEDED
THAT TWO THOUSAND DOLLAR MIRACLE LORD REMEMBER
HOW HE PROVED TO YOU ACCORDING TO MALACHI THREE TEN

> Bring ye all the tithes into the storehouse
> that there may be meat in mine house
> and prove me now herewith saith the Lord of hosts
> if I will not open you the windows of heaven
> and pour you out a blessing
> that there shall not be room enough to receive it

WITH THAT TWENTY DOLLARS THAT HE NEEDED AND THEN LORD
YOU TURNED AROUND AND BLESSED HIM WITH TEN THOUSAND
I SAID "LORD I'M ASKING YOU TO DO
THE SAME THING THE SAME TYPE OF MIRACLE
FOR MY DEAR FRIENDS IN CHRIST AT THIS ADDRESS"

Dear Prayer Family
Yes I do have personal problems
and I want to learn how to meet these PROBLEMS
through PRAYER and ask that God will

bless me with more "Good Fortune" in life
through your new SPIRITUAL PACKAGE
Here is the "Blessed Faith Handkerchief" back
I've slept on it for "1" night and
I've printed my name in the middle of it, by faith.

> *And God wrought special miracles by the hands*
> *of Paul so that from his body were brought*
> *unto the sick handkerchiefs or aprons*
> *and the disease departed from them*
> *and the evil spirits went out of them*

NOW WHEN I GET THIS HANDKERCHIEF BACK FROM YOU
(WITH YOUR NAME ON IT) I AM GOING TO TAKE
THIS VERY SPECIAL "FAITH HANDKERCHIEF" AND PRAY
FOR A SPECIAL MIRACLE FOR YOU. I AM ASKING YOU
TO HELP US WITH OUR IMPORTANT MINISTRY
AND TELL US WHICH OF THESE PROBLEMS ARE AFFECTING YOU

1. I have a financial need in my life
   I need God to bless me with some money
      for a certain need

2. I have a personal need in my life
   Someone has hurt me
   I have a physical need in my body

3. Someone is worrying me and troubling my mind

I AM ASKING YOU RIGHT NOW TO GET OUT FIVE DOLLARS
AND GIVE IT TO THE WORK OF JESUS CHRIST

Dear Reverend I requested a prayer that my husband
stop drinking It happened I'm so happy Thank Jesus

Dear Reverend My daughter has changed and is living
a new life in Jesus and service to the Lord

Dear Reverend In my prayer request I asked
for my job back Thank God I got a new one better

Dear Reverend My two boys got saved and one
filled with the Holy Ghost Praise Jesus

YOU WILL NOT NEED IT AFTER TONIGHT
RETURN IT TO ME IN THE MORNING I REPEAT
DO NOT KEEP THIS "FAITH HANDKERCHIEF"
AND PLEASE DO NOT BREAK THIS FLOWING OF GOD'S
SPIRIT FROM MY HOME TO YOUR HOME
RUSH THIS "FAITH HANDKERCHIEF" BACK
FOR I MUST WRITE YOU SOMETHING IN THE SPIRIT
THAT'S COMING TO YOUR DOOR
                    I'M ASKING YOU

3 Where the Green Gulf

Someone is worrying me and troubling my mind.
Shall I tell you about her?

They had the Christmas spirit,
went out partying till late.

> *Where the green Gulf*
> *slops out of its shallow dish*
> *praise sands for tilting up*
> *to contain it, Praise!*
> *Where somehow roadbuilders*
> *let go the cutting of live oaks*
> *curse the trees*
> *that crowded in at the curve*
> *and caught the car*
> *when it swung wide, Move*
> *your lips in a curse!*

I thank God she died fast
and didn't suffer or become
a vegetable, like they say.
But it was bad luck, real bad.

> *Where the green Gulf*
> *sloshes over sand and jetties.*

Someone is troubling my mind
who once used to go with me
to fish from the far end
of number six where the channel
is not too far out
and the good fish will bite.
Someone that used to come, too,
that liked fishing, out there
at the end where there wasn't
usually many others, someone

I took there when she was little—
she'd drop a string in the water
raw bacon tied to the end
and would bring up a crab
real slow so it wouldn't
let go and she'd get
sunburned and wear my hat
and now it's her that's worrying me
and I pray she's found her rest.

(I feel like I need
someone to turn to
to get over this sorrow,
Lord, to be full
reconciled with Your will
that took her away
when I hadn't ever thought
that she wouldn't live
beyond my days
that seem too long now
being longer than hers.)

> *Where the shallow Gulf tips*
> *in its bowl with each wave*
> *the water studies its way in*
> *through pilings, under the pier*
> *the ripples cross and crisscross*
> *like a thick reflected light*
> *that smells cold against*
> *the summer heat, smells of*
> *fish and creosote and floats*
> *the frail shells toward shore*
> *then pours back into its bowl—*
> *where the Gulf does this,*
> *and some praise its mild green,*
> *a man rests in the hard sun*
> *and wipes his face with a handkerchief*
> *that falls from his hand and's gone.*

And the water troubles him, sure,
but the most troubled is his will.
What he wishes he'd had is luck,
and not even for himself.
But luck just makes his misery
seem to come from some past mistake
that he can't remember making,
that's been punished past the mark.

4 Just Crazy Thinking

He didn't like being caged up.

went into the bedroom, put a .30-caliber

He had a real deep-down-inside
meanness, just like my dad.

boilermaker's helper, his emotions

I think it was just his coming up
through all those years, not having
any real person you could look up to
and trust and talk to and respect
what they say to you.

his emotions in tatters, went into the bedroom

He was impulsive.

Winchester rifle against his chest

He told me he was a burden
to me and my wife. I told him
that was just crazy thinking, you know,
my brother's keeper and that kind of thing.
He thought, with people having
to take care of him like that,
he was a bum, living with us.
Really, he wasn't.

"Goodbye trouble," said the note

I just laughed it off, you know.

Someone has hurt me

I told him that was just crazy thinking.

A few days before, in a fit

He had a real deep-down-inside
meanness, just like my dad.

in a fit of apparent rage he drew
a hunting knife across the girlfriend's

I just laughed it off, you know.

the girlfriend's name on his arm,
cutting the flesh so deeply
that he destroyed the letters of the tattoo

"I love you both very much
"so don't forget about me OK.

and pulled the trigger

"I'm sorry if I scratched your gun
"and I'm sorry I had to use it

put a .30-caliber Winchester rifle

"but it was all I could find for a week.

against his chest and pulled the trigger

"I would like you to do me
"a favor I know you don't like her
"but for me. Tell her I love her
"very much. I love you all.

When his brother

"Goodbye trouble."

When his brother and sister-in-law
returned, the television set
and the lights were on

I don't think he understood what
he was doing, that it would be permanent.

I have a personal need in my life

lying on the edge of the bed
with both feet on the floor
the rifle between his legs

He was impulsive.

bullet hole in his chest

5 READ THIS

THIRST IN THE LORD WITH ALL YOUR HEART
     AND HE WILL ACKNOWLEDGE AND HE WILL LIGHT
       THE WAY.
THIS PRAYER HAS BEEN SENT TO YOU FOR LUCK:
IT HAS BEEN AROUND THE WORLD NINE TIMES.
THE LUCK HAS BEEN BROUGHT TO YOU.
YOU ARE TO RECEIVE GOOD LUCK, WITHIN FOUR DAYS
     OF RECEIVING THIS LETTER.
THIS IS NO JOKE YOU WILL RECEIVE IN THE MAIL.
SEND A COPY OF THIS LETTER TO PEOPLE YOU THINK
     NEED GOOD LUCK.
DO NOT SEND MONEY.
DO NOT KEEP THIS LETTER.
IT MUST LEAVE YOUR HANDS WITHIN NINETY–SIX HOURS
     AFTER YOU RECEIVE IT.

AN HFS OFFICER RECEIVED $90,000.
DON RILLIST RECEIVED $59,000 AND LOST IT
     BECAUSE HE BROKE THE CHAIN.
WHILE IN THE PHILIPPINES GENERAL VOLEN LOST HIS LIFE
     SIX DAYS AFTER RECEIVING THIS LETTER.
HE FAILED TO CIRCULATE THIS PRAYER.
HOWEVER BEFORE HIS DEATH HE RECEIVED $795,000.
PLEASE SEND TWENTY COPIES AND SEE WHAT HAPPENS
     TO YOU ON THE FOURTH DAY.
THE CHAIN COMES FROM VENEZUELA AND WAS WRITTEN
     BY SOL ANTHONY DE CACIAF A MISSIONARY
     FROM SOUTH AMERICA.
SINCE THIS CHAIN MUST MAKE A TOUR OF THE WORLD
     YOU MUST MAKE TWENTY COPIES IDENTICAL
     TO THIS ONE AND SEND IT TO YOUR FRIENDS
     PEOPLE AND AXQUAINTANCIES.
AFTER A FEW DAYS YOU WILL GET A SURPRISE.
THIS AFTER, EVEN IF YOU ARE SUPERSTITIOUS.

TAKE NOTE CONTAIMO DIAZ RECEIVED THE CHAIN IN 1953
HE ASKED HIS SECRETARY TO MAKE TWENTY COPIES
AND SEND THEM, FEW DAYS LATER HE WON A LOTTERY
FOR 2 MILLION DOLLARS IN HIS COUNTRY.
CORL CRODULT AN OFFICE EMPLOYEE RECEIVED THE CHAIN
HE FORGOT IT AND IN A FEW DAYS HE LOST HIS JOB.
HE FOUND THE CHAIN AND SENT IT TO TWENTY PEOPLE.
FIVE DAYS LATER GOT AN EVEN BETTER JOB.
COLIN HOUCEILA RECEIVED THE CHAIN AND DOUBT BELIEVING
HE THREW IT AWAY, NINE DAYS LATER HE DIED.

DO NOT SEND MONEY
DO NOT BRAKE THE CHAIN.

6 Sermon of the New Preacher

You will ask me, then, What *are* the things of the spirit? Even the fire on the hearth, I tell you, the morning light, and cleanliness, and gratitude, and the mother's love of her small child, and the pattern in the leaf or wing . . . All things not material; as has been said.

That is why even the incarceration of some of you may be a spiritual experience, it will remove you from the material, I will hope, as much you as the monk who chooses to be confined.

But without commandments and a new heart, neither confinement nor a show of goodness is anything more than a useless feeding of delicate fruits to the ravening bloodthirsty dog of your brute snarling, your unkindness, your meanness, your lack of feeling, your blindness!

You have committed crimes and already you are caged and you do not know it!

But Brother, you say. Brother, I have needs, I'm in trouble, or I'm in pain, or I have sorrows and worries and wounds! I'm in debt, and my son won't straighten out, and my wife doesn't love me the way she once did, Brother, I'm talking about me!

But I'll tell you, when the flames have risen up roaring but a brief while through the dry wood, and died again, and the orange coals waver and glow under a small hot tongue of fire, that is the fire of the spirit.

When brick upon brick is piled until at the summit a great building ends and the air begins again, that is the air of the spirit.

When you look in the morning mirror, well-disposed to yourself, or at odds with yourself and striving against yourself as if you were an enemy to your own heart, and suddenly you see a spider retreat behind the mirror that you knew not had spun a web so brazenly in the household, to draw its web across your very face! —that is the spider of the spirit.

When after housework and day-labor you angrily taunt and torment each other you're so weary, and as you speak your shadows move across the cold wall which they do not touch or in any way change, that is the movement of the spirit.

And when the athlete's tired body sleeps and he dreams of his father, or she dreams of her mother, and weeps in the dream, that is the cleansing of the spirit.

I will not tell you some end of man is nigh, why do I need to tell you? We are each of us the end of man, the end of all men and women. And the beginning which is the beginning of the spirit.

I will make a list from A even unto Z of your wicked acts and your puny unavailing confessions and alibis, and I tell you the truth, I do not hold great hope for you.

You hop and dance from one thing to another and leave everything unfinished or done poorly. You wake in haste and you sleep in haste, you will even die in haste! Don't be surprised by it, or feel you weren't warned!

You have too many of everything and not enough of anything.

You mind leaps off like a fly from what it should dwell upon and instead of quiet thought you want rowdy commerce and loud clamoring, you cannot get enough of them.

Do you think there will be another life for you in which to take your time and do everything over again properly? Do you think killing a weak little impulse of good that is struggling in you for life is no more than killing a fly?

You are in the air, I tell you, leaping over a chasm that is bottomless, and even if to you it seems pretty narrow, it is far wider than you think.

You are like a mosquito that hovers against a confining window screen for hours because with its eyes smack against the fine mesh it cannot see the gaping hole above it through which it could easily pass.

You are like a leaf in autumn that, mistaking its fall for a moment's flight, thinks it will rise again when later it puts its mind to it.

Oh I could preach to you, but I won't anymore.

I won't sharpen anymore my pencils against you.

I won't anymore close my door and sit down at my desk of wood.

I won't anymore toil at the word.

I won't anymore put on robes and climb the steps to the pulpit, I won't anymore raise my voice against you, or for you.

I won't anymore wait for you at the door to clasp you as you leave.

I will take off my robes and retire into the world.

I will keep silent and use my hands for some good work.

When I see you I will turn my back to you.

I will reject your promises and apologies.

I will smash the dovecote and despoil the garden that I made for you.

I will not warn, I will judge.

I will not teach or console, I will punish.

Or so I say I will do. Do not test me, please, any further, Brothers. Plead no more with me, Sisters. I have said what I can say, and what I can do, I have done; no more can I add to either.

Let us say an amen, now, and go.

7 *Witness*

I had a funny feelin when the phone rang.
　　　"Dja hear me shootin?" my neighbor said.
　　　"No, Jim" —it's half a mile— "not a 'thang."
"Za big rattlesnake, uz in the shed,
　　　must be six feet if it's an eench,
　　　Ah got it with muh .22, one shot, come on fore the crowd."
"OK," I said, "but I'ze jist about to peench
　　　off a loaf, then I'll be over."
　　　It's like when somethin bad is a cinch
ta happen, an you feel like time's never
　　　goin to start up again,
　　　it makes you wanta run for cover,
that's the way I felt when I sat down
　　　on the toilet for a minit or two.
　　　I'd have to go on ta his place an by then
he'd of called everbody he knew
　　　an stopped traffic and somethin bad ud happen.
　　　An it did, too, cause this biker come through
lookin for trouble, seem like, all bint
　　　outa shape cuzza this buncha people
　　　in the road blockin iz fast way for im
an he got pissed off and beeped
　　　iz liddle horn an started pushin um back
　　　with'z bike till he looked up
an Jim uz holdin iz snake up high, it uz like
　　　somethin *happened* to im when he saw it,
　　　he went kinda crazy cuzza that snake,
an tried ta run down this kid
　　　who'z about ta cut the rattles off
　　　for Jim, an this biker barely hit
iz brakes an turned a liddle, jist enough,
　　　an people are yellin at im, he's about *so*
　　　close ta catchin it, but he's actin tough,
he says, "I coulda hitcha if I'da wanted to, ya know,"
　　　"Yeah, you jist try it," Jim says, cause
　　　now he's picked up iz *shotgun,* it's always loaded,

this biker pulls out a pistol an blows
    the snake in two, layin there, an then points it at Jim,
    but that's his mistake. Because
you won't take another shot at *enny*thang
    if you don't hit whatcha want to first,
    an Jim already had iz gun up an bang
the guy went flyin off iz bike with'z chest
    shot away an hit the road dead an iz bike
    fell over an that was it, it happened so fast
you could still hear the shot, it uz like
    one a those thangs you do as a reflex
    without thinkin, you're psyched,
ya know? —An then ya think, God A-mighty, it's Texis,
    ya just shot and killed the guy
    an you're not sure now *what* to expect.
About a dozen widnesses'll all say
    it wadn't exactly your fault
    but they *seen* ya do it in the lighta day.
You may be guilty even if you don't *feel* some guilt.
    Well here came the depitty sheriffs all at once
    from the county, an got Jim and everybody felt
awful when they put the biker's worthless body in the am-bu-lance
    an drove off leavin iz blood still on the road.
    That boy with the knife took the rattles, since
nobody else cared about em, an Jim's dog growled
    at me when I rolled the dead man's bike away
    into the shed where the *snake*'d been, my God, like iz life ud
keep goin and he'd be back for it someday,
    an I don't know what he died for,
    an I don't know why,
but it seemed like a thang that couldn't be helped, no more
    than it could've been foretold. They just ring
    in my head, both those shots, till I'm sore
with the sound of um, it uz a bad, wrong,
    needless, wasteful thing, with no lesson in it,
but by now *somebody* on this road has wrote a song
    about it probly, it'll come on the radio in a minit.

8 The Snarling Dog

Brother, have you heard them speak
of the recent quarrel between two sisters
who tore at each other's hair and eyes
till both were blind and bald last week?
An awful crime, and which is to blame?
    Brother, I was there.

Did you know in the morning paper it said
that two city gangs have stormed and warred
through the streets all month, and both so scared
they couldn't quit to count the dead?
And for what kind of fame?
    Brother, I was there.

You heard, I guess, about the school
where the brute teachers terrorized
the children and tore their tiny prize
hearts out of childhood with threats to kill,
after sexual torment and acts of slime?
    Brother, I walked by that school unaware.

In this hospital nearby—did you already hear?—
they've got a case of two little boys
dying of burns all over their bodies
who painted themselves and then caught fire.
Where was their mother and dad at the time?
    Brother, I wish I'd been there.

In some other country we sent our soldiers to
the place blew up and one young man
waited holding just a hand in the ruin

till finally it clawed his and went limp and let go!
(He himself suffered wounds and is lame.)
        Brother, they shouldn't've been there.

        That's what it's come to, we're told,
        behind the playground gate there's a snarling dog,
        he's everywhere, he leaps at your leg
        and gets it and won't let loose his hold.

        The snarling dog is in your locked car.
        The snarling dog's in your medicine chest.
        He'll tear at the hand you make a fist
        then he'll jump out again from your nightstand drawer.

        He can spring full size from a crack or a crumb.
        From the pages of your book he'll attack on sight.
        He's waiting in the garage shadows at night.
        When the TV picture comes on, it's him.

        An old lost lady will look frail and slight—
        it's the snarling dog dressed in her rags.
        You hand your money to the checker for your bags
        and the dog will thrash out of one and bite.

        The snarling dog is in bedrooms and halls,
        it walks the roads from dark till dawn,
        then it gets up again and goes on,
        slavering through barracks and ballfields and schools.

        He breaks in at night leading thieves and assassins
        and raves through the house, mauling the children.
        He attacks funerals and puts cold dread in
        everyone by leaping up onto the coffins.

Brother, I've seen him and I've come to warn
because he's on my trail, not a minute behind.
You'll see, believe me—you too will find
you're running to pass the warning on.

Have you heard people tell of the danger to us all
when this one's elected or that one breaks jail?
It's twice what you heard anyone tell
and they got the snarling dog on a chain at heel.

9 Cash or Turtle or Heaven

Just beyond that big sign for Ebenezer Church?—
you know the one—and Ellsworth's Polled Herefords?—
I had to swerve to miss a turtle in the lane
and I looked in the rearview and I saw the pickup
behind me, that was loaded too high anyway
with old furniture and all, swerve in order to
hit the damn thing and I hope it set
the sonofabitch back about five lifetimes.
Lindy sitting next to me, all she could
talk about was getting new sunglasses, like mine,
said she wanted the Zodiac ones, though,
so she could personally express herself, *her* sign.
What about you? Do any camping? Like to fish?
I just can't get away much these days, I'm short of cash.

~

The boss knows what's best for you, you don't
have to ask him for anything, he already
knows what you need, so every morning you should
hunch over your coffee and say this prayer:
Our father, which art
in business, incorporated be thy name.
Thy profit come, thy will be done,
at work as it is in Congress.
Give us this day our daily wage.
And extend our credit, as we have had
to give you those benefit concessions.
And lead us not into grievances or strikes,
but deliver us from unions: for thine
is the profit, and the power, and the lobby forever. Amen.

~

But I never will have all the cash I need.
That's a hell of a thing, that turtle, isn't it?
I hit a goddamn deer once, it broke
the windshield and smashed the fender in
like it was tinfoil—surprise you—I had it made
into sausage, though, and we ate that
for a whole winter. That was even before
I lost my job. Could use the meat now,
even getting it that way. And before Lindy
started going back to church with the kids.
I don't like to go much, I wasn't raised to it
like she was, don't see the point. If there is
a heaven, they got to keep some of these
goddamned bastards out of there, I say and believe.

10 In the Violent Ward

Like patients walking down
a windowed corridor sunlit from one side,
through trapezoids of light,
through the cold bars of shade,

we can't be sure we want to get well—
once you go out, time starts again,
your wounds may heal
and you'll want to wound someone.

All violent people secretly desire
to be curbed by something that they respect.
It can be the law, or their own children,
or the zodiac; it can be an ice pick.

It's so they may become known
to themselves. (But none of us
is known to another, we can't be.)
And not to be more like brutes but less.

And when not curbed, turning lethal and mad
they may rage till the last little bit
of anger is drowned, then they're mild
with the blood, they're pure, they're quiet.

But they'll hurt you still, you hear?
Stay away from them, they're bad.
They're waiting for some glorious mistaken expected one
and if you're not him you're dead.

They're waiting for what it is
that they'll respect; but they can't imagine
what it will be, they're afraid to know.
And till it comes to them, gentle or mean,

they'll still be sick or wounded,
afflicted somehow to be put in here
in these hallways and rooms, edgy with
this stale whispering we do, in this drugged air.

I mean with us: here where we all
spend our days walking, unfit,
wondering who among us may put steel
into another; who holds the whip; who needs to feel it.

From *The Ruined Motel* (1981)

In the Kingdom

The lamb's head was caught,
it had butted its way
at the squared fence-wire
till it pushed through
and was held. We thought
for a moment, remembering edgy courtesies
when we had trespassed before.

This was where the wind and a stream
had hidden a little valley,
and one farm, at the foot of steep
pastures, lay in the deep fold.
We had seen the hills and fields
tilt, as we walked, into a green
perfection, and when we'd looked up

we'd tripped in midair—
watched a hawk come
leap the crest above us with
two wingbeats and whistle
over the sheep, floating level
with our eyes as the combe
dropped away deeper and broader.

The hawk scanned the hillsides,
and near us in a small grove
starlings crackled like lighted tinder.
Invisible as angels, we waited—
far below, a toy man and dog moved
from house to barn, and cattle under
a mossy roof were lowing.

And there before us was
the lamb—tugging at its own head
in jerks, snared inside
its field by a blind five-yard

fence-spur near the gate.
The ewe stood at a distance, answering
the high bleats, marble-eyed.

I called out and waved to the distant man,
who didn't see or hear me.
Then I climbed in, the ewe
balked and dodged away as I took hold
of the lamb, which leapt with fear
till I could push the ears down
and with a hard shove back the head through.

It staggered and fell,
tottered up, ran off and banged
into the ewe. It pulled at a teat
but was led straight down to the flock,
all of them jumpy and dull.
I came back over the gate
and you took my arm in yours.

As if loosed from a tether
the hawk rose, then—cupped a gust
in its wings and banked, slipped over
the far hill, following a hedge.
The farm tucked itself further
into its fold with each step
we took toward the village

and disappeared behind us when
the lane turned, cut the slope,
under sparse elms, and sank a foot more
into the red earth. Then came the schoolyard,
the little houses, gradients
marking the descent, each roofline
lower than the one before.

And our door, which led
into a happy solitude that year.
Looking at the map, we talked of the stream
called Healeyes, and the place with a name
meaning "a muddy ford." *Reg,* you said,
much later, when we were quiet,
What was it like to touch the lamb's head?

The Voice of Someone Else

I've lived under this big porch a long time.
Where you are—where you breathe
and talk and things come to hand—
is above me: warmth, painted wood, prospects. . . .
But I like this lattice-shadow better.
(You may remember now, with a chill,
how you caught a glimpse of my eye
on you, from in here, but it doesn't matter
what you think you saw in the checkered light—
fine skin and jewels, or a curved beak,
or fur, or scales that rustled as they disappeared.)

I am my own keeper. I have lost nothing.
Every old thing is with me—the afternoon
when the field burned, and the good belt
with the turquoise buckle, and the long game
under the lights. . . .
But also the stories that your sister told
her friend when no living thing was listening.

When I come up, it's by a passage
inside you, to look out through
your eyes, that are mine any time I want.
Likewise your body, likewise your soul.
The things that rouse me?
Hurt, strength, good weather, bad weather,
accidents, secrets being told, secrets
held back, and then, knowing—
this comes from far off, calling me from above—
that the hand is holding a pen.

for William Goyen

BREATH

I remember coming up,
pushing off from the bottom
through dull ringing silence
toward the undersurface of the water,
where light sparkled—or patterns
fanned across roof-fabric:
that deep comfort, long ago, of
being carried to the house
in the dark, half-asleep, only
half-interrupting the dreams
that had made the car a craft
among stars. But the air—
and the house—held
depths, too, where someone else,
someone larger, locked the doors,
did late-night chores and turned out
the lights, too tired now
to stop the inevitable
fight, rising to it. . . .

Underwater, you hear bodies
burble over you, smashing the sunlight—
and voices in other rooms begin
to swell, drawers shutting, bags
slammed down from closet shelves,
footsteps. . . . Till a child's fear,
held under, shudders free, floating up
to explode with a gasp, and splashes
out of sleep, and he sucks air,
and discovers that nothing
consoles, there is no air,
there is no waking, not anywhere.

THE DAYS

Up first, alone, only you
caught the earth dipping
just before dawn into silence.
The cars waiting outside
glistened in the dark with dew.
Then a mockingbird would go back
to the song it would break with a buzz,
and through the walls you'd hear
a few early workers, taking
the shortcut down our street,
gun it coming out of the S-
curve and leap into third for
that straight quarter-mile to the stoplight.

Pulling the door shut behind you
at six, by yourself on the porch,
you left us still asleep to fall
with the weight of the day
toward bottom, where we'd come
in late from an aimless, hours-long
cruise in the Fairlane and go softly by
your bed at midnight to the bathroom.
In a scratchy chatter two commentators
would be tallying late-season
farm-team hits and runs
from the floodlit stillness
of Busch Stadium. Then
the studio insomniac's voice—
that all-night call-in debate on divorce,
gun control, drinking . . .
till the produce and livestock prices
came on at five and you were up.

"LUCKIES"

A loop of rusty cable incises
its shadow on the stucco wall.
My father smiles shyly and takes
one of my cigarettes, holding it

awkwardly at first, as if it were
a dart, while the yard slowly
swings across the wide sill of daylight.
Then it is a young man's quick hand

that rises to his lips, he leans against the wall,
his white shirt open at the throat,
where the skin is weathered, and he chats
and daydreams, something he never does.

Smoking his cigarette, he is even
younger than I am, a brother who
begins to guess, amazed, that what
he will do will turn out to be this.

He recalls the house he had
when I was born, leaning against it
now after work, the pale stucco
of memory, 1947.

Baby bottles stand near the sink inside.
The new wire of the telephone, dozing
in a coil, waits for the first call.
The years are smoke.

LENTILS

Ezra Pound again

You still appear
to test me, interrupting
the line and knocking
it apart—though I can't
be sure it's you.
From so far off, coming at me
out of books and other people's mouths,
you're far less real than
the old woman from Lodz
who forgot who I was
when she was eighty,
I fifteen.

Your silence, and hers.
Your madness, that was
not charming, not fruitful.
And hers, her fear:
her speechless thorazine stare
as, on some inner screen
that she thought
sheltered her from us
who had loved her,
she watched the steady
image of some one thing
she could remember—perhaps as you
in the Washington asylum
had thought of the paper clips
rusting in your desk at Rapallo.

When she spoke to herself
did she say we didn't love her.
She could tell.

So she still appears to me, still strong,
to test me, scolding and correcting—
posture, English, piano.
The faint faint accent and scent of age,
and on the stove behind her—
forgotten for the moment—
the steaming pot of lentils.
No, no. Try it again.

THE LETTER

A scene remembered: the car
stopping, a back door opens, four
figures slowly climb down in the dark,

too frightened to speak, put out
as a punishment, and the damp night
finally shuts us up
like a chill hand slapped over
our bickering and complaints.

We held onto each other, forlorn
little circle, our backs to an infinite
black canebrake, and whimpered
as the tires scuffed through
soft dust and rumbled away.

Then nothing . . .
The drone and flutter and deafening throb
of the world, one small light
burning far away atop a derrick.
We had no hopes,

could barely draw breath to sob
till the car crept up again,
headlights off. No one of us would
break the grip of another to get in.

And I tell myself: we have
a pact, ever since, never to let go.
But that timid dance, hands
locked in passionate fear,
ends today with a letter: "One
curious thing. I remember the horror
of being driven away in the car while you
alone . . ."

So I look at my hands. They are empty,
and the cane thicket whispers in the wind.
When the car comes back, the ten-year-old boy—
the oldest—talky, thin, vain, wanting
too soon to reason and argue, will look in
at the startled man and woman,
the three children, and turn away,
a stranger of thirty, unable to speak.

When the car comes back.

SMALL ELEGY

Someone has left us now
before we have even touched.

Getting lost in the pity of it
sweeps you into an unknown stretch
of canyon where oars thud
against rock and rip free of your hands, you clutch
at help, and even though
you save yourself, the river
funnels through the gorge
and roars, roars, roars.
Regret, a backwash of pain,
one lost life swirls down rapids,
rushes away, out of reach.

It's not forgetting that you want—
it would be easy to drop
one shoulder and dive, to come up
gasping in a car on the way to work
or blue in the face over the dishpan,
staring for who knows how long
at a cup scoured clean under the suds.
And not remembering.

But the absence that is born
must live as long as a man or a woman.
There: invisible it comes headfirst,
a bloodstreaked nothing, and is flushed away.
While in the white room the dry light
is cold; and waiting to be taken home
mute ghosts lie in a row of empty cribs.

At Noon

The thick-walled room's cave-darkness,
cool in summer, soothes
by saying, This is the truth, not the taut
cicada-strummed daylight.
Rest here, out of the flame—the thick air's
stirred by the fan's four
slow-moving spoons; under the house the stone
has its feet in deep water.
Outside, even the sun god, dressed in this life
as a lizard, abruptly rises
on stiff legs and descends blasé toward the shadows.

HOPPY

Ancientest of cats, truest
model of decrepitude,
you shamble and push your own
sloppy shape across the room,
nosing the floor in your slow
unhappy step-by-step, and
with dollops of baby food
splashed around your whiskers, on
chin, on snout, and in one scarred
ear, don't you think it's gotten
crappy, this life, now the years
have slipped by, old Counselor?
You mop the rug with your tail,
you slap a tired paw against
the door, and turn dim yellow
eyes, flecked with a weariness
of having seen so much, back
over your jutting shoulder
to the faces that study
the exquisite mishap or
the dopey luck that has left
it to you—of all the world's
mopes and most unlikely wise,
prophets and poets—to stop
the bored chatter of these frail
merely human types and top
all their tiny much-boasted
perseverances with your
pained apocalyptic glance.

THE RUINED MOTEL

Give the mourning doves any sun
at all and they will begin to grieve.
Their song, riding the steam that poured up
from the snow on the window-ledge,
came in to us as we scanned
the damp wreck of a seaside room,
all the things no one inherited:
the sour pink and beige paint,
a throng of water-stain shapes
on the walls—splotchy heads
and moldy animal herds—and behind us
brown vines leaning in at the door
to greet the webs and frost-burnt
mushrooms in the closet.

We sheltered there while our car
held alone the whole weedy expanse
of asphalt fronting the ocean,
and we listened to the cold wind
spill through the sea-grove and splash
against the line of downed carports
and the crowd of pines in the pool.

Looming ahead of us
at the end of the empty road, the shell
of the place had made us think
that it must have been ugly
even when new. Maybe ruined
it suits the small outpost of worshippers
nearby at Immanuel Baptist Church
(Fundamental and Independent),
who grasp their tradition with such force
they tear it apart, their fierce
conviction shredding the creeds
while doves coo and with a useless hiss

the sea bites into the beach-snow
and falls back across the crescent sands.

I was thinking, This was where we had brought
the nation, to neighboring new tries
either abandoned or shuddering inward with extremes—
till you said to me, The ghosts in this place
are unhappy. Then I too could hear them—
couples revenging the hours they had
together under ceilings
that never fell on them, the too-loud talk
at dinner and the hedging hopeful
postcards in the morning.
We stepped away from them, from the boards
and slats of their collapsed beds,
from their fatigue, from musty air and dead wires,
we went back into the salt wind
and the noisy swaying pines, out
of that heap of winter-storm
tide-wrack. We didn't want to make
any mistakes but those we could say were ours.

But in that time we stayed there
we took the loss into ourselves,
obsessed with it—not stones
but rotting beaverboard and cold snake-nests,
not columns but dark hallways half-floored with sand.
And if the light that fell on us
as we walked toward the water,
that warmed our bones and stirred the doves,
made the scene seem a lesson-book—
the angles of human spaces, the path
upward—what did we read?
Under light-shafts from broken clouds,
an immense illumination
of breached walls, frail trees,
a narrow road, snow on the dunes,

dry weed-wisps and bright bits of plastic . . .
and rolling in the waves
like heads that strove
against their own deformity
the great whelks
dashed and battered till hope
was the hollowness in their cold clean skulls.

PRAYER BEFORE BATHING

Meat-fetor of a dog's breath;
the *tristeza* of a striptease;
an old man's gurgling rattling cough
that shakes him so wildly
he holds his sides and walks
in step with his convulsions
till they cease and he spits
on the sidewalk; blood
and gold dust on gauze
under the patient's hand,
where a surgeon had to cut
her ring away from the wound;
the old woman who sees the clock
reading 2:05 and in a little
girl's voice, a singing voice,
says loudly, "It's exactly
two o'clock!" and looks around
the room for an answer;
and every hope,
every book, ends with money;
and they say that the terror
in fairy tales is good for you;
and the priest walks slowly
across his campus and bends to pick up
each bit of stray paper and trash
on the path till with delicate
resignation he drops
his handful into a barrel;
and after the census,
when they take our names from us,
we must wash.

THOSE WHO ARE GONE

Have I betrayed your memory?
                              How many times!
The days pour down in a river, and a few trim boats,
well-used to work and cared-for well, float toward sea
alongside green slime and wrack in the muddy dregs.
If storms have drummed the banks upstream
more ruin descends—the water heaves and drags
its spoils under thumping ash-gray clouds
that flash with thrusting fire.
I say nothing, I offer no excuse. But other waters
rise silently from springs, drop by drop, seep up
from an unfathomable source to brim rock troughs,
then spill from crags and pinnacles, and thud
and burst and rush beneath the blue,
over clean stone. Those waters call your name forever.

After Antonio Machado

From *Roofs Voices Roads* (1979)

Two Promises

Spring will come back
along the route winter took,
touching things inadvertently and changing them
the way someone
I did not know I loved
unthinkingly laid
a hand on my arm
while speaking to another.

~

And autumn comes down along the river
and passes through town
on its way south,
heads for places it will never reach,
leaves everything
perfectly placed, bare and clean:
the line of poplars at the streambed,
our lives.

BETRAYAL

A hot afternoon
Saturday's sun through leaves and shattered on water
old men buying ice cream from vendors along the park wall
and inside, the children's zoo and people walking paths

So we took a bus
rumbling uptown to the museum and then strolled
high and cooler on the winding shaded way
A small escape was possible, we thought

But no—
Pressed in among the crowds, we moved to watch the unicorn
fall before the hounds
Looking out from the heavy graying cloth
its shining eyes seemed to stare on us alone

And the tiny jewel
set in trappings of age seemed to cast its faceted eyes on us
while at our backs hunters moved
and for a moment we became tapestry
and the jewel watched us and was alive

And yet you more than I
felt before the triptych   looking inward at the altar
and before the jewel and the unicorn's dead eyes
the web closing

You began
to move a little faster   to quicken in the shadow
of the fear of capture that floated down on us like nets
or frames changing us from us to portraiture

I was not so quick to see
An arch in the cloister took the curve of your head
kept in stone your bending grace and motion

and not until you turned and saw me shaping you
did I know my gaze too was cage was net was shadow

Dusk

1

The sound of a clarinet, all alone, comes from
the next farm down:
Mozart's concerto.

Solitary reed, the player is insane.
Kept home
by her family all her life.

2

Or a creature living
in the depths of the sea, finally
tossed up dead onto the sand.

What could have survived such an existence?
It is impossible to imagine
anything coming out of this single, empty shell.

3

And in the hills it was
the gold-miners' heedlessness that
exposed bedrock beneath the thin soil.

Just so I bare too much
in the attempt to attract love.

4

Reflection on the living-room window-glass
has put the potted ivy & geranium out in the street.
A man strolls through them with his dog.

His chest is in flames.
What a relief to see the fire of loneliness
there too, breaking

from another man's heart!

for Anne Hall and Ted Haas

IN A STUDY OVER A STAGE

Laughter, then shouting,
downstairs in the little theater
while rain drubs in these gutters;
the fluorescence spreads
like bloom
on this hard wood table.
Applause rattles it:
raw wood, as if the pelt had been pulled
off and the aching heart
lacquered with love and hatred.

Now empty seats and silence:
the lamps burn barely smoking;
everything suspended.
Hard wood, smooth wood,
how did you come to lie so stolidly
over uproar and passion?
The actors retire, even they sleep
on worn planks, but far from the timberyard
and the shrieking blade.

PINE ISLAND

The day ends at the end of land,
the Gulf of Mexico as placid as a stone.
The sunlight gathers the gold-green wall of trees
in pleats, and the shaded folds steam
with a soggy, mentholated scent. . . .

In the tiny asphalt lot, a blue Ford stands ticking
beyond the cold slabs of the picnic tables.
The man sits with the battered door open
on his side, and the tired woman leans over
the wheel, silently toying with the keys.

"You're the one brought me here, to this
West Coast, two years," he says,
and spits; then his lungs pull
on the rope that is knotted at his lips
in a cigarette. He spits again, and a slow
bell peals erratically on a buoy offshore.

"Two years wasted," he says to the Gulf.
"Shit. Not any more, no thank you, not for you
or anybody else." The sun has chosen
a lane of useless glory, and it takes it
to the end, letting the whole of west
Florida pull away, plentiful and savage.

She has not spoken a word
as he continues to talk too loud and not
to her, one thin leg dangling out,
a polished shoe near the crushed butts.
A dog, a little dog, half-blind and hairless,
rises between them on the front seat, facing back,
eyes bulging at the mainland palms.

BUDDY

Daylight waddles to the horizon's
squat roof-peak like an iguana.
We travel.

Oak, pine, catalpa,
the boughs of bright leaves
spin their coins into the air

and vanish, the ground
swims up around us bearing
its acres of rice.

Then banana and palm fronds
marshal the streets toward water.
The lizard

lazes now in mid-heaven.
As if crazed, you drive the car
into lumbering flight

from pavement to sand, where it lunges
and shies through the shifting ruts
till we hit firm beach,

careen along beside the waves.
We stop.
You have taught me heartlessness

and swagger, and how to rig up
for surf. I walk in,
sinking, arms high, and wade

to chest-depth, standing
on the back of a sandbar
that is sidling, with us astride,

down the shore. . . . The fish
strung from my waist tug listlessly
at me, bleeding into the murk.

A sharper tug,
and I see the small hammerhead
turn and surge

for more. Heaven's lizard gapes
and light pours from its jaws.
Fear fills my mouth

like water. I tear the stringer
from me, flail toward shore
against the water's grip.

I call for you.
You hear me, you see me, you
laugh and raise your right arm

above the water,
leaning back. The iguana
quivers with aimless rage.

You cast the lead and bloody bait
high into the air,
ready to hook the sun.

Behind the Mountain

Late in the evening
we lay awake, the only
ones awake there, but
stunned, half
blacked out by the vast
size of the building
we were to sleep in:

                  stories
and stories rising from
rubble, from the fields
of parched grass
of dust and dereliction
on the outskirts of the city,

lay awake listening
for hours to the water
dribbling from the tap,
the switch
engines struggling
late at night
to ready the long
trains for dawn.

Zagreb, 1971

In Memoriam Ezra Loomis Pound

A midland
>   peninsular light
"Mediterranean"
>   hugs the white stucco

>   and heat
rises, rearing up from cool dawn and earth
into its midday passion
>   for precise description:

leaves mesh like knives
or woven wire,
narrow black shadows lie scattered in a prison
of limbs and leaves

and recall other places,
recall the effect of other places

on the traveler, striding through Spain
and southern France, whose works

lie on the shelf
like a basket of lemons and stones.

California, 1973

An Archaeology of the Future

You can dig up the bones
of the mistakes we are making,
they are buried in the air
overhead. You can feel
the chill that will hold
its breath forever after today,
it seals all our prophecies
in vaults, all wrong.
But it is no task
to foretell the future: it appears
as an exported tractor
rusting in a reed shed, the hush
after tropical rain has fallen
on uncompleted highways. And here,
where our dreams shine so brightly
we think they are clouds,
the world we are not
ready for surrounds us, and it is
wasted, and we cannot use it.